ENDORSEMENTS

"In the Christian church, there are those who have their wheelhouse or lane. I call them specialists. There are the apologists. There are those in the political realm. There are the creationists and the scientists. And then there is Seth! Seth Gruber is the leading voice of the pro-life movement. There's no one else out there like him. He is a Ben Shapiro and a Charlie Kirk, all wrapped into one for the pro-life movement.

Seth's book *The 1916 Project* is shaking the foundations of hell. I believe the battle for the lives of the unborn will define the future of the United States of America. And, in these Last Days, this book may very well be the thing God uses to awaken His church from her slumber and finally end the genocide of babies. If there's one pro-life book you read, make sure it's this one!"

Jack Hibbs
Senior Pastor of Calvary Chapel Chino Hills

"*The 1916 Project* is everything the Church needs to know about how this evil and sinister culture of death was created. I wish someone like Seth had written this book in the 1970s and discovered all of the dirty little secrets about the sexual revolution we're dealing with today. We need more men like Seth in the church, educating and equipping the family of faith to stand like a bulwark between our children and the forces of darkness. This book is the wake-up call we need as a sleeping church! Read it now and join us in the fight!"

Kirk Cameron
Actor and Television Host

"Seth Gruber is one of the most important pro-life voices in America. This book lays out the path toward abolishing abortion. Read it to find out how."

Charlie Kirk
Founder of Turning Point USA

"Seth is the most articulate, fearless, and passionate pro-life speaker I've ever heard. I meet believers all around the world who want to know what happened to American culture and what can be done to change our crash course. Seth has written the definitive guide to how we lost our culture. Never have I read a more comprehensive, well-researched, and spiritually illuminating book on abortion and our hyper-sexualized culture. If the church awakens and ends abortion in America, this book will be cited as a spark that lit a fire in the hearts of Christians to finally end this great evil."

Nick Vujicic
Motivational Speaker and Evangelist

"Not since researching my best-selling book *Bonhoeffer: Pastor, Martyr, Prophet, Spy* have I been so surprised at the things I did not know. Seth Gruber has magnificently answered the questions of every concerned Christian in our sick, out-of-control culture: What is happening to our country? How did we get here? And what can be done to stop the demonic madness? Seth has unearthed and exposed innumerable facts about the history of today's "progressive" movement. *The 1916 Project* brings astonishing clarity—and bombshell truth. Thoroughly documented and cited, this book will be viciously attacked by the Left because it exposes PRECISELY what they've been trying to hide from us. Please read it!"

Eric Metaxas
Best-selling Author, Speaker, and Host of the *Eric Metaxis Radio Show*

"If you don't want to get upset, bothered, heartbroken, angry, disgusted, or forced to face how you will respond to genuine evil—then you shouldn't read this book. It has affected me. At times, I wanted to punch a wall. At other times, the rage took the form of weeping. Prophetic, rousing, shocking—a slap to the face of the apathetic man."

John Cooper
Co-Founder, Lead Vocalist, & Bassist of Skillet

"In the midst of a looming crisis in the ancient world, Mordecai said of Esther that she was born for just such a time as this. Similarly, this book and the meticulous research of Seth Gruber has arrived on the scene of yet another looming crisis—and it is precisely what we need for such a time as this."

Dr. George Grant
Pastor Emeritus of Parish Presbyterian Church
Author of *Grand Illusions: The Legacy of Planned Parenthood*

"This book by Seth Gruber is a biblically-inspired, historically-grounded summons to the conscience of God's people to fight abortion. Read with an open mind and heart; it will reveal to you that the biggest challenges to defeating the culture of death are not the enemies around us, but rather the ones within us—cowardice and excuses—often dressed up in religious garb. Our most urgent need is not to figure out what we must do, but to summon the courage to do it. This book has me jumping up and cheering! Read it, and let's go fight for life!"

Frank Pavone
Pro-life Leader, National Director & President,
National Pro-life Religious Council, Priests for Life

"Seth Gruber is one of the brightest young lights in the pro-life movement. He is incredibly well-read and has a quick mind that allows him to connect the dots of the culture wars in a way that few can match. *The 1916 Project* is his latest work, and I recommend it highly to anyone who truly desires to understand the underpinnings of the culture of death and how we got where we are as a society."

Anthony Levatino, MD, JD
Former Abortionist

"I thought I pretty much knew all the pro-life answers, having been raised in a pro-life home with a dad who baptized Norma McCorvey, the Jane Roe of *Roe v. Wade*, and spending most of my life ministering at abortion clinics. Then I read this book. Seth Gruber brings theology, history, philosophy, and storytelling together like few other thinkers in the pro-life movement. I couldn't believe some of the mind-blowing facts behind this fight that I'd never heard before! This is a must-read for every Christian, including those who think they've heard it all!"

David Benham
President of Cities4Life

"The Church now faces unprecedented challenges in a secular age. *Roe's* demise opens the door to resolve the abortion debate within the States via the democratic process—through elections and laws. Our national debate over abortion is anything but over. Followers of Jesus must work to ensure every unborn child has the right, protected by law, to take his or her first breath. In this important new book, Seth Gruber combines thorough cultural analysis with a biblical worldview of the sanctity of human life, pointing us to a model of Christian cultural engagement that is faithful to the gospel. Gruber offers a timely vision for the church—a vision that is desperately needed in the twenty-first century."

Dr. Robert J. Pacienza
Senior Pastor of Coral Ridge Presbyterian Church (Fort Lauderdale, FL)

"What's behind the growing insanity of our culture, and why are most Christians silent in the face of it? Seth Gruber exposes it all. But I warn you: If you just want to sing your hymns louder to drown out the cries all around you — the cries of children being mutilated and executed in the name of choice—you don't want to read this stunning, succinct, and brilliant book. It might motivate you to redirect some of your Netflix time to restoring civilization for your children and grandchildren. Gee, I wonder what Jesus would do?"

Frank Turek, Ph.D.
President of CrossExamined.org
Author of *Stealing from God*
Co-author of *I Don't Have Enough Faith to Be an Atheist*

"I've made it my mission to follow God's will for my life and a massive part of that has been traveling the world, defending the most innocent and vulnerable—His unborn children. I am honored to share this pro-life fight with Seth Gruber who is making waves during an ever-growing crisis against the unborn. This book is not just profoundly accurate, but it's a must-read for every adult no matter where they stand in this battle. After reading this, please give a copy to a friend who may have a different viewpoint. Seth's words will ignite the urgent fire inside each one of us that God has been calling us to courageously rise up against and fight."

Abby Johnson
CEO of And Then There Were None and Prolove Ministries
Former Planned Parenthood Clinic Director, Author & Speaker

THE 1916 PROJECT
THE LYIN', THE WITCH, AND THE WAR WE'RE IN

SETH GRUBER

The 1916 Project

Copyright © 2024 by Seth Gruber

All rights reserved, including the right of reproduction in whole or in part in any form, except for brief quotations in printed reviews, without prior permission of the publisher.

Unless otherwise indicated, all Scripture is taken from THE HOLY BIBLE, NEW INTERNATIONAL VERSION®, NIV® Copyright © 1973, 1978, 1984, 2011 by Biblica, Inc.® Used by permission. All rights reserved worldwide.

Scripture marked ESV is taken from The ESV® Bible (The Holy Bible, English Standard Version®). ESV® Text Edition: 2016. Copyright © 2001 by Crossway, a publishing ministry of Good News Publishers. All rights reserved.

Publisher Information
Vindex Media, Inc.
PO Box 284
Ottawa, KS 66067

For more information or to contact the author, please email contact@thewhiterose.life

ISBN 979-8-9905948-0-7 (softcover)
ISBN 979-8-9905948-1-4 (hardcover)
ISBN 979-8-9905948-2-1 (eBook)

Cover design: 1924US

Editorial Team: Dr. Mark Tuggle, Penny Tuggle, Cristina Wright

Interior design: Ben Wolf, Inc.

Publishing services provided by BelieversBookServices.com

First printing: 2024

Printed in the United States of America

To my wife Olivia:
whose faithful love, prayers, and unceasing support
have kept me in this fight long past when I would have failed

ACKNOWLEDGMENTS

We are all the recipients of the deposits people have made in our lives, which whether we recognize it or not, have made us who we are. It's therefore impossible to acknowledge and thank every person who deserves it, and whose sacrifice and service have resulted in this most timely of all books. But acknowledgments are still in order. Here are a few...

My wife Olivia, without whom neither this book nor my ministry would exist. You sacrifice more than I see and deserve more thanks than I can give. Slaying dragons and raising dragon slayers with you is truly the greatest adventure.

My parents, whose patient and faithful presence and teaching prepared me for this culture war. My mother, who bravely chose to homeschool me before it was popular and grew gray hairs far earlier because of me. My father, whose consistent love and prayers I've always taken for granted, and unlike many dads, was always there.

My godfather Gregg Cunningham, whose trailblazing courage in the fight for life has helped alter the personality of the pro-life movement in ways he likely doesn't even know. I've gone from peeing on you as an infant to interning for you in high school and college. Your fearlessness and resolve are contagious and prepared me for the fight I didn't know I'd have at a Christian college.

Scott Klusendorf, whose book *The Case for Life* changed my life as a senior in high school. Thank you for taking me on as a graduate, fresh out of college, and foolishly confident. Your guidance, mentorship, and phone calls did more to shape a restless twenty-four-year-old than you know.

Jack Hibbs, my earthly hero. My life changed on October 11, 2020. For some reason, you let an almost unknown twenty-nine-year-old step into your pulpit. And my speaking schedule has been packed and overflowing ever since that Sunday. You blessed and affirmed a calling God put on my life and got fully behind it. I learn more from watching you live out your Christian walk than anyone else in my life. One of my spiritual fathers, you have ninja-level discernment and courage, and I hope I can be like you when I grow up.

Rob McCoy, the giver. Attending a church in Orange County in 2020, I was frustrated and wondering if my family would ever find a church that felt like home. Then I met you. Three months later, I moved my family to Thousand Oaks and joined Godspeak Calvary Chapel. Without being asked, you opened your home, your heart, your network, your wallet, and your pulpit. My family and I were home, with people who weren't content to condemn evil from the bleachers. I will always call you my pastor.

George Grant, the smartest man I know. A lion of the faith and an expert on more topics than anyone I've ever met; your speeches and books have done more to shape my understanding of our culture war than anyone alive. Always a text away, your wisdom, guidance, and friendship have become some of the greatest joys of my life.

CONTENTS

Introduction	xv
1. Whitewashing the Witch	1
2. The Unholy Trinity of Depravity and Death	13
3. The Theological Roots of Evil	29
4. 1916 and the Race to Destroy the "Unfit"	47
5. 1916 and the Sexual Revolution	65
6. Woke As Wolves	85
7. The Divine Trajectory of God's People	109
8. The White Rose Resistance 1.0	129
9. Saved but Not Salty	141
Afterword	155
Notes	157

INTRODUCTION

"A man who has nothing for which he is willing to fight, nothing which is more important than his own personal safety, is a miserable creature and has no chance of being free unless made and kept so by the exertions of better men than himself."

—John Stuart Mill

I've been a pro-life activist since I was a fetus.

It's true. My mother was the director of a pregnancy resource center in Azusa, California, while she was pregnant with me. As pro-abortion advocates like to say, "My body, my choice." So, according to them, the baby (me, in this case) was just a clump of cells, or "pregnancy tissue"—whatever that is. And if there was just one body, whatever my mother did, I did. All those babies she rescued during those nine months? That was me too.

But even without using nonsensical progressive math, I have been a pro-life activist for as long as I can remember. My mom's passion for saving the unborn was contagious, and I grew up understanding that the millions of unborn babies being sacrificed on the altar of self is a national nightmare. There was no separating my Christian faith from my opposition to abortion. The way I saw—and still see it—is if a person truly loves Jesus, he or she will love the most vulnerable in our society: the unborn.

Most people don't spend a lot of time thinking about abortion, about what it means to terminate a pregnancy, especially when they're young. But I did. I was homeschooled until ninth grade when I entered Whittier High School in Los Angeles County. It was then that I realized I didn't always have a good answer to objections from friends who were pro-choice. So, a few years later, I decided I would do my senior project on the subject of abortion. Not only would I have to do my research, but I'd also have the opportunity to present the pro-life position to my classmates.

Not long after I made my intentions known, the administration quietly told me I couldn't present on the topic of abortion. When I asked why, I was told, "There are just some topics we don't allow, and this is one of them."

I was a teenager, but I wasn't naïve. I knew this was a clear case of discrimination because I had chosen a topic that makes progressives uncomfortable. I also knew I had a First Amendment right to speak on abortion if I chose to do so. I retrieved a copy of the Constitution I had been assigned to read for government class. "Have you ever read this?" I asked my faculty advisor. "I recommend you do. Because you're about to have a lawsuit on your hands."

That's right—I threatened to sue my high school for viewpoint discrimination. And do you know what? The administration immediately backed down. It just goes to show that when you stand up to bullies, they usually fold like a piece of paper. There are people who will rule over us if we allow them to. Sometimes, all it takes is good people who are willing to stand up and say, "Sit down!" to set them straight.

I gave my presentation, spoke the truth to a room full of my peers (plus teachers and administrators), and left high school knowing I had stepped into a calling. I would speak up for those who can't speak for themselves, and I would do everything I could to rally others to the cause. A culture that butchers babies is a sick and twisted one, but most people are asleep. They don't know they're sliding ever so comfortably into hell. However, history bears this scenario again and again. The only thing to do is wake people up. I hope I can do that.

After graduation, I enrolled at Westmont College in Santa Barbara, California. Being a Christian school, I might have expected a bit more support on the pro-life front. But no. As I quickly learned, Westmont doesn't take an official position on the issue of abortion, and the school employs faculty members who are openly pro-abortion. The school says it believes the Bible to be the Word of God, but apparently, the board and administration officials are fine with ignoring passages like Psalm 139:13–16, which says:

> *For you created my inmost being;*
> *you knit me together in my mother's womb.*
> *I praise you because I am fearfully and wonderfully made;*
> *your works are wonderful,*
> *I know that full well.*
> *My frame was not hidden from you*
> *when I was made in the secret place,*
> *when I was woven together in the depths of the earth.*
> *Your eyes saw my unformed body;*
> *all the days ordained for me were written in your book*
> *before one of them came to be.*

Of course, I wouldn't let a simple thing like ambivalence toward the murder of millions of babies deter me. I founded the school's first pro-life club on campus and was president of that club all four years of my college career. As an initiative of that club, I tried to invite the Genocide Awareness Project to come to Westmont and put up one of their displays.

During my senior year of high school, I was an intern for the Center for Bio-Ethical Reform, which sponsors the Genocide Awareness Project. When I first started, they had me spend two full days scanning images of aborted babies into their database and categorizing them for various educational projects. Up until that point, I had never really seen what abortion does physically to a child. Of course, I *knew* what abortion does, but I had never seen images before. When I did, things changed. I started believing that if people saw the evil of abortion with their own eyes, they would have a hard time rationalizing any position that would uphold abortion as good or even acceptable.

Westmont's pro-abortion professors were fine with policies that allow a mother to mutilate the child growing in her womb, so there should have been no problem showing what that looks like with images seven feet high by fifteen feet long. But, of course, they did. People who proudly champion abortion with their voices typically hide when confronted with the consequences of their position.

For three years, I petitioned the administration at Westmont to allow the Genocide Awareness Project to come on campus and put up one of their displays. And for three years, I was denied. So, during my junior year, I decided to do it myself. I didn't have the printing power to create larger-than-life displays, so a few friends and I made our own signs, each of which featured a graphic image of a baby's body parts post-abortion. Then, we stood outside the dining hall with our signs one morning.

Within an hour or two, two administration officials approached us and asked if we had received permission to stand there with our signs. With my GoPro camera recording, I told them no, I didn't have permission, but I also didn't need it. I had read through every page of the student handbook, and there was nothing in the bylaws or school covenants prohibiting me from exercising my freedom of speech in this way. I wasn't out there as an official representative of the pro-life club; I was just a tuition-paying student exercising my First Amendment rights.

After about two hours of debate, the director of student life told me, "Seth, you may not be breaking any rules, but I do believe you're disrespecting us." I responded, "And I feel like you're disrespecting the murdered children in Santa Barbara who are probably killed at a higher rate by students at this university than anywhere else in this city. It's happening on your watch, and you have professors here who champion it." That was the end of our discussion, so my friends and I showed up outside the dining hall with our signs several times over the next few weeks.

I tell you all this to let you know what you're getting into. I believe the problems with our world today, especially concerning issues of life, are not the fault of evil men and women. After all, you can't blame evil people for being evil. The real reason our society is in the mess it's in is because, by and large, good people have remained silent and polite and have not stood up to challenge the progressives in their midst who want to draw our nation further away from God, from commonsense truth, and the precipice of our own destruction. They'd rather play it safe, get along, and be nice than stand up and cause a scene.

But here's the thing: the world doesn't change if you're afraid to stand up and be strong. The Marxists, the Leftists, and the pro-abortion cultists know this, and they're more than happy to stand up and shout their views over the heads of the masses who disagree with them. You've seen them do this, and you've probably wondered how we got here.

This book is a little bit like those signs my friend and I held up outside of the dining hall at Westmont. Its purpose is to confront you with the truth. Our nation and our world didn't get to this sad state by accident. It was by design. We'll trace the progressive movement and the culture of death, especially as it relates to the unborn, back to 1916 when Margaret Sanger illegally opened her first birth control clinic in New York City. We'll expose the connections between Sanger, the eugenics movement, the Nazis, and modern phenomena like Black Lives Matter and pornographic sex education in public schools.

Like those signs, the purpose of this book is not to shock you (though it may do that) but to recruit you. I hope to rouse you to action, to inspire you to join me in making a scene, speaking up, and proclaiming the truth, not just with your voice but with your life. I'm not being dramatic when I say the future depends on it, for if we do nothing, the darkness will keep growing. Twenty years ago, no one would have imagined we'd be debating how much pornography is okay in an elementary school library or whether or not it's a good thing for a teenage girl to chop off her breasts and have an artificial phallus surgically attached. No one thought we'd ever see people condemned simply for being white or other people cheering for infanticide legislation. But here we are.

If we don't act, where will be in another twenty years?

CHAPTER ONE
WHITEWASHING THE WITCH

"Just as loss of memory in an individual is a psychiatric defect calling for medical treatment, so too any community which has no social memory is suffering from an illness."

—John H. Y. Briggs

Down Bleecker Street in the heart of Manhattan, there's a building like a thousand others. From the outside, it looks benign. Without its sign out front, you wouldn't know that within its walls thousands of innocent lives are snuffed out each year. The brick façade keeps the world from seeing the mutilation of small bodies. Those horrors are reserved for the back rooms, far from the busy sidewalks and streets.

Abortion clinics are not unique to New York City, of course. But this "health center" is special. It's holy ground for those who uphold the sacrament of abortion as an integral part of their secular religion. This unassuming building houses the flagship clinic of Planned Parenthood, the world's largest purveyor of abortion on demand. For decades, the building was called the Margaret Sanger Health Center, in honor of the organization's founder. But on a warm Tuesday morning in July of 2020, Planned Parenthood of Greater New York issued a surprising press release, announcing that the location would be dropping "Margaret Sanger" from its name.

In the official statement, Karen Seltzer, board chair of Planned Parenthood of Greater New York said, "The removal of Margaret Sanger's name from our building is both a necessary and overdue step to reckon with our legacy and acknowledge Planned Parenthood's contributions to historical reproductive harm within communities of color."[1] The strange thing was that Margaret Sanger's racist and genocidal ideology was not some secret that recently came to light. It's been well-documented. Critics of abortion on demand and Planned Parenthood's targeting of African American communities have pointed it out time and time again.

In a famous letter to C. J. Gamble, a member of the Birth Control Federation of America, Sanger wrote of her intentions to deceive and decimate communities of color:

> It seems to me from my experience where I have been in North Carolina, Georgia, Tennessee and Texas, that while the colored Negroes have great respect for white doctors they can get closer to their own members and more or less lay their cards on the table which means their ignorance, superstitions and doubts. They do not do this with the white people and if we can train the Negro doctor at the Clinic he can go among them with enthusiasm and with knowledge, which, I believe, will have far-reaching results among the colored people. His work in my opinion should be entirely with the Negro profession and the nurses, hospital, social workers, as well as the County's white doctors. His success will depend upon his personality *and his training by us.*
>
> The ministers [sic] work is also important and also he should be trained, perhaps by the Federation *as to our ideals and the goal that we hope to reach.* We do not want word to go out that we want to exterminate the Negro population and the

minister is the man who can straighten out that idea if it ever occurs to any of their more rebellious members.[2]

These paragraphs are but the tip of the iceberg, a rare (but certainly not isolated) moment in which Sanger spoke candidly about her devices. However, if you were to trace the trajectory of Sanger's life, studying her influences, her associations, her actions, and her legacy—something we will do in later chapters—you would find that Sanger not only despised people of color, but she also saw the weak, the poor, and the disabled as useless members of society who should be placed in work camps or sterilized.[3] She spoke at Ku Klux Klan events and invited card-carrying Nazis to contribute to her magazine, *Birth Control Review*. She wasn't a complicated person with a few flaws; she was, by every true measure, a force of destruction and evil, a villain of the highest order.

And yet, for decades, the liberal establishment and the mainstream media have defended Margaret Sanger as an angel of light who liberated women and restored dignity to the poor. When Hillary Clinton was honored by the Planned Parenthood Federation of America with the Margaret Sanger Award in 2009, she said, "I admire Margaret Sanger enormously—her courage, her tenacity, her vision... And when I think about what she did all those years ago in Brooklyn, taking on archetypes, taking on attitudes and accusations flowing from all directions, I am really in awe of her."[4]

Sanger's own words were either ignored, as seems to be the case with Clinton's gushing remarks, or they were reimagined as part of an imagined right-wing conspiracy to defame the patron saint of abortion. Journalist Jennifer Latson claimed as much when she cited Sanger's famous line about "[exterminating] the Negro population" from Sanger's letter to Gamble and then proceeded to argue that the sentence, "in context, describes the sort of preposterous allegations she feared—not her actual mission."[5] In other words, according to Latson, Sanger was being sarcastic, and people on the Right simply can't take a joke.

Similarly, Gloria Steinem attempted to transform Sanger from a racist into a champion for African American equality: "She correctly foresaw racism as the nation's major challenge, conducted surveys that countered stereotypes regarding the black community and birth control, and established clinics in the rural South."[6] According to Steinem, all those abortion clinics in predominantly black neighborhoods were a precursor to affirmative action, a leg up for the disenfranchised.

These were the tactics employed by feminists and pro-abortion activists for years. They simply would not admit that Sanger embraced and promoted the eugenics movement or that she sought to destroy black communities as part of her crusade to create a utopian society void of undesirables. So, what happened in the summer of 2020 to make Planned Parenthood do an about-face and, in their own words, "acknowledge... [the] historical reproductive harm within communities of color" caused by their founder?

Black Lives Matter.

That's right—it wasn't pressure from pro-life groups, exposure from conservative political activists, or even Planned Parenthood's own employees calling out the organization's racism[7] that brought about this one-hundred-and-eighty-degree change. It was BLM Inc.

You may remember the media's laser-like attention on systemic racism in the summer of 2020 following George Floyd's death. If so, you may also recall the "mostly peaceful protests" that destroyed neighborhoods, brutalized the police, robbed businesses, harassed and murdered civilians, and set fire to American cities. It was in that supercharged atmosphere that Black Lives Matter became a household name.

These revolutionaries firmly believe that if an institution has racism in its history, then that racism flows through the DNA of the organization to this day. It doesn't matter how things have changed or what good may have been done in the intervening years. The rotten genesis of these institutions is all that matters. If the roots are speckled with racism, the whole tree has to be burned down. And they don't just mean that metaphorically—BLM activists brought physical destruction to communities across the United States.

According to the narrative being stoked by the mainstream media at the time, these protests (read: riots) were spontaneous and appropriate, the natural overflow of grief stemming from the "murder" of George Floyd at the hands of racist police officers. Our country is hopelessly racist, they told us. It's not just individuals either; the racism that has infected our nation since its founding flows through our most venerated and important institutions. What we saw in response during the so-called "Summer of Love" was good and right and perfectly just—and if you think otherwise, you're a racist.

The ethos of Black Lives Matter was not forged overnight, or even in a season. The groundwork for BLM was laid decades earlier through an unrelenting stream of progressive propaganda in academia, but it was cemented in the national conversation nearly a year before the unrest of the summer of 2020. In August of 2019, *The New York Times Magazine* published a series of essays entitled "The 1619 Project." The brainchild of Nikole Hannah-Jones, The 1619 Project is an attempt to recast American history as a tale centered on slavery, the first African slaves being brought to our shores in 1619:

> Out of slavery—and the anti-black racism it required—grew nearly everything that has truly made America exceptional: its economic might, its industrial power, its electoral system, diet and popular music, the inequities of its public health and education, its astonishing penchant for violence, its income inequality, the example it sets for the world as a land of freedom and equality, its slang, its legal system and the endemic racial fears and hatreds that continue to plague it to this day. The seeds of all that were planted long before our official birth date, in 1776, when the men known as our founders formally declared independence from Britain.
>
> The goal of The 1619 Project...is to reframe American history by considering what it would mean to regard 1619 as our nation's birth year. Doing so requires us to place the consequences of slavery and the contributions of black Americans at the very center of the story we tell ourselves about who we are as a country.[8]

"The 1619 Project" wasn't simply a one-off alternative history project designed to give the progressive readers of *The New York Times Magazine* something to discuss at cocktail parties on Martha's Vineyard. It came with a series of essays, podcasts, and a ready-to-use K–12 curriculum,[9] and its army of content creators was somehow able to pack in all the major creeds and priorities of humanism. The aim was nothing short of a social revolution. The project, in all its various incarnations, praises abortion, socialism, defunding the police, revoking the right to bear arms and reparations. Conservatives are blamed for pushing racism into every facet of American culture even though it was Democrats who supported slavery, passed Jim Crow laws, and fought tooth and nail to keep civil rights legislation from becoming the law of the land.

In the spring of 2020, as Anthony Fauci was busy telling Americans to wear two masks and stop attending church, Nikole Hannah-Jones received a Pulitzer Prize for "The 1619 Project" even though many historians—some quite progressive in their politics—pointed out that "The 1619 Project" was, in fact, terrible history. For instance, the project claims the chief aim of the American Revolution was to preserve the institution of slavery, even though many of our country's founding fathers were adamantly opposed to slavery. It also claims the Declaration of Independence was itself racist in its orientation while ignoring voices like Abraham Lincoln who saw the founding document as enunciating liberty for both whites and blacks.[10]

But it didn't matter. Objective history was never the purpose of "The 1619 Project." The goal had always been to mainstream progressive ideas and to upend American institutions—to tear down the nation as we know it so it could be rebuilt into a progressive wonderland.

Proponents of "The 1619 Project" argue that the bigoted spirit born in 1619 has swept through every nook and cranny of the culture, with no area of our society left untouched. It follows, then, that every aspect of our culture can and should be viewed through the lens of 1619. So, of course, nine months later after the Gray Lady's Sunday magazine birthed the project, when George Floyd died during a police altercation, progressives were salivating to shout, "Racism!" as the only possible reason.

As Black Lives Matter madness was consuming the atmosphere in mid-2020, Planned Parenthood found itself in a tight spot. Of course, Margaret Sanger founded the American Birth Control League, which later became Planned Parenthood, with an eye to decimating communities of color. Like the Klan members and Nazis she was known to pal around with, she was a white supremacist. If anyone would have said, without hesitation, that black lives *don't* matter, it was Sanger. And so, after decades of denial, misdirection, and outright lies, Planned Parenthood leadership could no longer stand with their matriarch. Sanger's name wasn't just removed from Planned Parenthood's building in Manhattan. New York City also eliminated her street sign on Planned Parenthood's corner, previously known as Margaret Sanger Square. She was discarded and trashed as though she was, herself, one of Planned Parenthood's everyday victims.

As Alexis McGill Johnson, president and chief executive of Planned Parenthood, wrote, "We will no longer make excuses or apologize for Margaret Sanger's actions."[11] That statement is itself a double-edged sword. Planned Parenthood, caving to the pressure of Black Lives Matter, owned up to Sanger's cruel history, but the organization also promised not to apologize for it either. In other words, they admitted the roots of their tree were planted in racism, but the tree itself would continue to grow unfettered.

It was an odd situation. According to every rational standard, Planned Parenthood and Black Lives Matter should have been in direct opposition to one another. One organization, allegedly, wanted to improve the lives of black citizens across this country; the other wanted to dismember the most vulnerable black citizens in the womb. Yet the two outfits forged an alliance of sorts.[12]

An ancient proverb states, "The enemy of my enemy is my friend." To accomplish an important goal, natural adversaries will find common ground and work together. These alliances are often eye-opening, for they reveal true motives. In the case of the unique truce between Black Lives Matter and Planned Parenthood in the summer of 2020, one thing became certain: both organizations' opposition to traditional American values, conservative principles, and historical Christian doctrine was far more important than the lives of preborn black babies.

As this book will continue to prove, revolution and liberation are all that matter. You may call it the Marxist revolution, the communist revolution, the secular moral revolution, the sexual revolution, or simply the humanist revolution; it's all the same thing. It's no coincidence, then, that the roots of both Planned Parenthood and BLM Inc. are fundamentally Marxist in orientation. In fact, BLM Inc. founder Patrisse Cullors has openly said of herself and her co-founder Alicia Garza, "We are trained Marxists." Both were mentored by avowed Marxist Angela Davis, a student of the Frankfurt School, whose founders and teachers essentially created the revolutionary strategy of the modern Left. They called it "the strategy of the robes." That is, if they could capture the robes of the courts, the robes of the clergy, the robes of the academies, and the robes of the scientific institutions, the revolution would be perpetual and no one need fire a bullet. An early member and eventual director of the Frankfurt School, Max Horkheimer, was not shy in explaining this strategy. He said:

> The revolution will not happen with guns, rather it will happen incrementally, year by year. We will infiltrate their schools and bureaucracies, transforming them into Marxist entities as we move toward universal egalitarianism.[13]

And no one perfected and implemented the "strategy of the robes" better than Margaret Sanger. She is likely the most effective progressive revolutionary in over a century, whose nefarious legacy and impact on our current culture is greater than any of her revolutionary forebears or protégés. The famous author and godfather of American liberalism, H. G. Wells, summed it up:

> Alexander the Great changed a few boundaries and killed a few men. Both he and Napoleon were forced into fame by circumstances outside of themselves and by currents of the time, but Margaret Sanger *made* currents and circumstances. When the

history of our civilization is written, it will be a biological history, and Margaret Sanger will be its heroine.[14]

Interestingly enough, the founders of the Frankfurt School fled Germany to escape Hitler, as many of them were Jews, and set up their school at Columbia University in New York City. They and their protégés became the fathers of the radical hippie movement and the radical yippie movement and thus helped architect the sexual revolution. They later became tenured professors at American universities.

Of course, Planned Parenthood and BLM Inc. are not alone. There exists today a network of unaffiliated yet fundamentally aligned institutions and associations hell-bent on remaking America into a secular, humanist, and socialist state. It includes everything from the legacy media to our schools, to Wall Street banks, and Fortune 500 companies. There is no hierarchy, no earthly general in the field giving orders across organizations to inculcate the culture, and yet these forces do communicate and coordinate. The strategy of the robes has worked, and we are naïve if we believe they're acting independently of one another or that the current state of affairs came upon us by mere chance.

The prophet Hosea ministered during a time of prosperity and decadence in ancient Israel. As the people ate and drank and enjoyed their shortsighted version of the good life, Hosea appeared on the scene to warn them of coming judgment for their idolatry and wickedness. As part of his indictment of the nation, he declared these words from God: "My people are destroyed from lack of knowledge" (Hosea 4:6a).

The priests, who had been charged with teaching the people God's ways, failed miserably in their task. They, too, had given in to the spirit of the age and had forsaken their responsibilities. So, the people were ignorant of God's commands. They didn't know about their calling as the people of Yahweh. They didn't understand the covenant their forefathers had entered into. They didn't fully comprehend the dark nature of the false gods they served. They didn't know where to place themselves in the story God has been writing since the beginning of time. Their lack of knowledge was their own destruction.

There are many people today who don't know who Margaret Sanger was or what her evil agenda was about. They don't know the roots of Planned Parenthood or the historical forces behind today's progressive movements pushing everything from infanticide to critical race theory, to ESG scores, to pedophilia, and to the mutilation of our children's genitals. You may be among them. But it is no longer—and never should have been—an option for Christians to stay in the dark, hoping for the best as our culture slides down the slippery slope to hell so fast it would make the residents of Sodom and Gomorrah blush.

G. K. Chesterton once wrote, "Happy is he who not only knows the causes of things but who has not lost touch with their beginnings."[15] In other words, "Happy is he who knows how we got here. Happy is he who can see the ancient, pagan, and—let's face it—demonic ideas that were planted in the cultural soil by political elites and the high priests of secular progressivism. Happy are those who know and choose to resist the tide of evil."

For too long, the church in America has been content to stay out of politics. We've spent our time building ministries of mercy and 501(c)(3)s to care for the broken people who have been shattered by the crashing waves of progressive culture when we should have been fighting upstream against these ideas and preventing them from infiltrating nearly every facet of our society in the first place. We have not understood the strategy of those who seek to do us harm, and as a result, we have not stood our ground as we should have. We have been lulled into a waking sleep, believing everything will simply work out, or worse—that some of the Marxist and humanist ideas that have overtaken our culture are not all that bad after all. If nothing changes, we will be like the people of Israel in Hosea's day: our lack of knowledge and our refusal to understand will be our destruction.

In the past few years, we've witnessed a public health crisis that was used to shut down small businesses and churches. Our youth experienced record-high levels of depression, suicide, and drug addiction. Federal mandates were written overnight to impede our medical freedom. Unelected bureaucrats weaponized federal agencies to crush their political opponents. Pastors were arrested for preaching and singing in public. Transgenderism was mainstreamed. Sexually explicit and pornographic curricula in America's public schools incited a peaceful grassroots movement of parents speaking at school board meetings, concluding with Attorney General Merrick Garland labeling such parents "domestic terrorists." States passed legislation allowing the government to "trans" your children without your consent. And this short list is just a selective recap of the Left's influence over the past several years. Needless to say, we are at a crisis point.

But there is good news. People who generally don't care about politics and would otherwise avoid the subject have begun asking questions. They are desperate to know what is happening to America. They want to understand how we got to this place. Tyranny overplayed her malevolent hand, and commonsense individuals and families have been awakened.

Having spoken to hundreds of thousands of people about how we got here, I have never seen such energy and excitement as I have in recent months. People want to learn, understand, and engage in the resistance against this culture of death. The number one question I receive from Bible-believing Christians is this: "Seth, what can I do?" The answer is straightforward: seek knowledge and understanding. That's what this book is all about—uncovering the hidden history and agenda of the progressive perversion sweeping across the United States and the world.

Hundreds of years before Hosea warned the Israelites of coming judgment, there were men from Issachar, "men who understood the times and knew what Israel should do" (1 Chronicles 12:32a). This group of two hundred leaders allied themselves with David as he sought to unite the twelve tribes of Israel under his kingship. Though the Bible doesn't tell us anything more about this group, what it does say with a few short words speaks volumes. These men set an example that's still relevant for us today. They took the initiative to understand what was happening in their moment, and they acted upon what they knew.

The decision to take Margaret Sanger's name off of Planned Parenthood's flagship abortion mill in New York City was an admission—an admission that the leadership of Planned Parenthood, and the Left in general, have been lying to you about their intentions and their history. Now is not the time to ignore what's been revealed. Instead, it is our moment to dig deeper and find out everything we can. We need to act in our day, to train up the next generation for the onslaught that's sure to come their way in the future. Like the men of Issachar before us, we need to be people who understand our times.

CHAPTER TWO
THE UNHOLY TRINITY OF DEPRAVITY AND DEATH

"To comprehend the history of a thing is to unlock the mysteries of its present, and more, to discover the profundities of its future."

—Hilaire Belloc

When the letter came in the mail, the first thing Leon Whitney noticed was the postmark. *All the way from Germany*, he thought to himself, not knowing who it could be from. He opened the envelope, unfolded the note, and read. Seconds later, he was beaming. His first instinct was to show the letter to his good friend and boss, Madison Grant.

Whitney served as the executive secretary of the American Eugenics Society, an organization that Grant had helped found. Both men believed the next great step in society's evolution would not come by some technological breakthrough or a second Enlightenment; it would come only when brave people like them took the necessary steps to make sure "the survival of the fittest" was not impeded by government handouts or Christian charity. It would be better still when those deemed "unfit" for a productive society were removed from the culture altogether.

A year prior, Whitney's article, "Selective Sterilization," had appeared in *The Birth Control Review*, a periodical popular among progressives, including many in Europe, as the letter in his hand attested. He had been invited to write for the journal by Margaret Sanger and her American Birth Control League, and his article "adamantly praised and defended the Third Reich's pre-holocaust race purification programs."[1] Whitney's writings were now growing in popularity in all the right circles, and he knew it. Still, this letter signaled that a new threshold had been crossed.

Upon arriving at Madison Grant's house, Whitney held out the envelope to his friend. "Our writings are influencing the Germans," he said. Grant smiled, then walked over to his desk and retrieved his own envelope, the handwriting on which was identical to the one Whitney had received. "I know." The signature at the bottom of both letters belonged to none other than Adolf Hitler. Though both men had received a letter from the Führer, Grant had a bit more to boast about, since Hitler had called Grant's book, *The Passing of the Great Race*, "his Bible."[2]

However, Whitney's work on eugenics caught Hitler's attention too. Prior to his letter from Germany's new chancellor, one of Hitler's staff members had written to Leon Whitney and "asked in the name of the Fuhrer for a copy of Whitney's recently published book, *The Case For Sterilization*. Whitney complied immediately."[3] Adolf Hitler was learning quickly from and absorbing the ideas of America's foremost eugenicists. In short order, the tables would be flipped and it would not be Hitler admiring America's eugenics leaders, but them admiring him and wondering why they could not be as quick and decisive in their preservation of the *übermensch*.[4] Leon Whitney admitted as much when Germany's sterilizations of the "unfit" exceeded 5,000 human beings per month. He said, "While we were pussy-footing around...the Germans were calling a spade a spade."[5]

In *The Passing of the Great Race*, Grant argued that Northern Europeans—those of the so-called "Nordic race"—were superior to all others, including lower-stock whites. Grant saw America as essentially a Nordic country but feared that, given enough time and the continuation of loose immigration laws, the Nordic race would slowly disappear, and the United States would enter an irreversible period of decline. Of course, Hitler was delighted with the premise of the book as it gave pseudo-scholarship to his ideals, and he saw in Madison Grant a kindred soul. The Führer was so impacted by Grant's book, which was published the same year Sanger opened her first brick-and-mortar Planned Parenthood clinic, that Hitler included entire sections of it in his book, *Mein Kampf*, with some sections seemingly plagiarized in their entirety.[6] Later, in 1936, three years after Hitler seized power, the Nazi Party listed *The Passing of the Great Race* as essential reading.[7] Here's a bit of what the Nazi leader thought was so wonderful in Grant's book:

> Mistaken regard for what are believed to be divine laws and a sentimental belief in the sanctity of human life tend to prevent both the elimination of defective infants and the sterilization of such adults as are themselves of no value to the community. The laws of nature require the obliteration of the unfit and human life is valuable only when it is of use to the community or race.[8]

To understand just what sort of soul Grant was, we need to visit the Bronx Zoo a few decades before the infamous Hitler letters arrived in the mail. There we would find a young man named Ota Benga in the monkey house. His appearance was striking. Being a member of the Mbuti pygmy tribe from the Congo, he had dark skin and only rose to a height of four feet, eleven inches. Believing Benga to be less than human, Grant lobbied the zoo to put him on permanent display as a sort of Darwinian missing link.

In that era, Grant was not a lone monster. Many influential progressives shared his mindset. Consider this editorial from *The New York Times* about Ota Benga:

> The pygmies…are very low in the human scale, and the suggestion that Benga should be in a school instead of a cage ignores the high probability that school would be a place… from which he could draw no advantage whatever. The idea that

men are all much alike except as they have had or lacked opportunities for getting an education out of books is now far out of date.[9]

There was, of course, some measure of controversy with the exhibit. African American clergymen protested loudly. As a result, Benga was allowed to roam the grounds with a bit more freedom than he had before, though he was still considered a zoo attraction. Visitors verbally and physically taunted Benga, and he responded in kind. And so, to avoid further violence, the zoo eventually released Benga. But the emotional and psychological damage had been done. About a decade after his stint in the Bronx Zoo, Benga borrowed a gun and took his own life.

Today, just the mention of the words *Nazi* or *Hitler* evokes images of gas chambers, Holocaust trains, and untold suffering. But back in the early decades of the twentieth century, before people could see Hitler's path dead-ended into a pile of bodies a mile high, his ideals were in vogue on both sides of the Atlantic. Eugenics was seen as the solution to society's ills. Remove the infirmed, the handicapped, the mentally ill, and the low-IQ rabble, and such people would no longer be a drain on limited resources.

At the center of the American push for policies that favored the principles of eugenics was an unassuming office in New York City, where Madison Grant, Leon Whitney, and others attempted to change cultural attitudes through the American Eugenics Society. Not by coincidence, on the same floor of the office building where Grant and Whitney advocated for a society void of undesirables, was Margaret Sanger's American Birth Control League. Margaret Sanger and Madison Grant were friends. They wrote for one another, raised funds for one another, participated in one another's conferences, and even shared office space. So closely knit were their two organizations that Whitney suggested their monthly publication simply merge with Sanger's *Birth Control Review*. Whitney wrote, "It would be an excellent thing if both the American Birth Control League and the American Eugenics Society used the same magazine as their official organ, especially since they were *both interested so much in the same problems.*" After meeting with Sanger about this possibility, Whitney reported to his colleagues that "she felt very strongly about eugenics and seemed to see the whole problem of birth control as a eugenical problem" and when asked about combining their publications, he stated, "Mrs. Sanger took very kindly to the idea and seemed to be as enthusiastic about it as I was."[10] In truth, Sanger's vision only varied from Grant's and Whitney's by degrees. In her own words, "Eugenics without birth control seems to us a house built upon the sands. It is at the mercy of the rising streams of the unfit."[11]

Before concepts like eugenics and forced sterilization of certain "lower" populations went out of fashion, Margaret Sanger was a champion of these hell-formed ideas. She swam in the same cesspool as men like Lothrop Stoddard and Havelock Ellis (more on them later), but given the widespread influence of Planned Parenthood and the culture of death she promoted throughout her life, Sanger descends to a lower circle with Charles Darwin and Adolf Hitler. Sure, Sanger's image has been managed well by her disciples and minions, so she often escapes the condemnation Darwin and Hitler receive for undermining Western civilization. But it's hard to deny how she and the organization that she founded helped bring about the culture we have today.

This chapter is something of an evidence board with pins and strings connecting Sanger to all manner of foul creatures. And as much as her supporters would like to distance her from Darwin and Hitler, the three form something of an unholy trinity, a united front of depravity and death.

Sanger had been a warrior for the cause of eugenics years before ever meeting Leon Whitney or Madison Grant. In her 1912 book, *The Pivot of Civilization*, she wrote:

> There is every indication that feeble-mindedness in its protean forms is on the increase, that it has leaped the barriers, and that there is truly, as some of the scientific eugenicists have pointed out, a feeble-minded peril to future generations—unless the feeble-minded are prevented from reproducing their kind.... Every feeble-minded girl or woman of the hereditary type, especially of the moron class, should be segregated during the reproductive period. Otherwise, she is almost certain to bear imbecile children, who in turn are just as certain to breed other defectives.[12]

Segregation camps? I know. It's shocking. Most of us would never have had any idea these are the talking points of the founder of Planned Parenthood. I could have cited this quote as coming from Joseph Goebbels or Adolf Hitler, and I bet you would have believed it. The activist media would never want us to know these detestable ideas were spewed forth by the patron saint of feminism herself.

In the first decade of the twentieth century, Sanger had been a part of the labor movement in Greenwich Village. As an advocate for workers' rights, she mingled with Marxists and socialists and was heavily influenced by their ideas. One Marxist concept, in particular, resonated with Sanger: moral people tend to be immune from revolutionary thought. Therefore, society will only change if sexual and social mores are destroyed. The social revolution must begin with a sexual revolution.

Sanger understood that if you could titillate the masses, slowly breaking down their inhibitions and shattering any moral compass they might carry, they would be easier to control. That is, sexual liberation is political control. Sanger was refining the strategy of the robes so well that while almost no one knows the names of the founders of the Frankfurt School, almost everyone knows the name Margaret Sanger. In 1914, she published her first magazine, which lasted for eight issues. It was an eight-page pamphlet entitled *The Woman Rebel* and carried the slogan, "No Gods, No Masters." In the first issue, she wrote,

Why *The Woman Rebel*? Because I believe that deep down in woman's nature lies slumbering the spirit of revolt. Because I believe that woman is enslaved by the world machine, by sex conventions, by motherhood and its present necessary child-rearing, by wage-slavery, by middle-class morality, by customs, laws and superstitions. Because I believe that these things which enslave woman must be fought openly, fearlessly, consciously.[13]

As I mentioned, Sanger's first magazine only lasted for eight issues. That's because, in August of 1914, she was indicted for breaking federal anti-obscenity laws, which prohibited sending contraceptives, abortifacients, or sexual content of any kind through the US Postal Service. Of course, *The Woman Rebel* qualified as sexual content, since Sanger was quite graphic in her descriptions. And that was the point. She was attempting to challenge social mores and carve a new path for mainstream American sensibilities.

Rather than face the charges brought against her, Sanger shipped her children off to stay with friends and shipped herself off to the United Kingdom. For a year and a half, she lived in self-imposed exile, but her time in England didn't soften her ambitions or even curtail her radical ideology. Instead, she only grew more convinced of her path as she mingled with revolutionaries on the other side of the pond.

Sanger joined several socialist societies and communist groups and became enthralled with neo-Malthusianism. Named for the early nineteenth-century scientist Thomas Malthus, Malthusianism is the idea that while the human population grows exponentially, food production cannot. Therefore, mass starvation is inevitable. Rather than simply waiting for enough years to pass until people go hungry, neo-Malthusians believe it's better to do something ahead of time to thin out the population and avoid the inevitable suffering that will come when food supplies run short.

In his magnum opus, *An Essay on the Principle of Population*, Thomas Malthus wrote the following:

All children born, beyond what would be required to keep up the population to a desired level, must necessarily perish, unless room be made for them by the deaths of grown persons...

Therefore...we should facilitate, instead of foolishly and vainly endeavoring to impede, the operations of nature in producing this mortality; and if we dread the too frequent visitation of the horrid form of famine, we should sedulously encourage the other forms of destruction, which we compel nature to use. Instead of recommending cleanliness to the poor, we should encourage contrary habits. In our towns we should make the streets narrower, crowd more people into the houses, and court the return of the plague. In the country, we should build our villages near stagnant pools, and particularly encourage settlements in all marshy and unwholesome situations.

But above all, we should reprobate specific remedies for ravaging diseases; and restrain those benevolent but much mistaken men, who have thought they were doing a service to mankind by projecting schemes for the total extirpation of particular disorders.[14]

Knowing the sort of world Margaret Sanger had already been busy advocating for—and where her path eventually took her—it's not difficult to see what she appreciated about Malthusian thought. She became a true believer. For Western civilization to continue, "the physically unfit, the materially poor, the spiritually diseased, the racially inferior, and the mentally incompetent had to somehow be suppressed and isolated—or perhaps even eliminated."[15]

If Thomas Malthus's argument is true—the human population will always outgrow food production—the only logical conclusion is to embrace eugenics, which is precisely what Margaret Sanger did. Eugenics is the practice of selective breeding to improve a population's genetic composition. This is done by sterilizing or killing human beings who have been deemed unsuitable for society.

Drawing from Darwinian thought, proponents of eugenics in the first half of the twentieth century did not believe all races were equal. Instead, the "bad" races must die out to make room for the "good" ones. The "bad" races were generally those who were poorer, darker, and more infirm than the proponents of eugenics. Is it any wonder, then, that years later, when Sanger's abortion clinics began dotting the busy streets of America's cities, they primarily landed in communities of color?

While in England, free from the confines of marriage and children, Sanger became something of a nymphomaniac, sharing her bed with men like H. G. Wells, George Bernard Shaw, and Arnold Bennett. She also began a lengthy relationship with a physician and writer named Havelock Ellis.

A strident proponent of eugenics, Ellis was also a strident proponent of every sexual deviancy that had ever popped into his sick and twisted mind. He was known to stage elaborate orgies, and he even enticed his wife Edith to embrace lesbianism so he could watch. Throughout his miserable life, Ellis published more than fifty books covering nearly every aspect of sexual attraction and perversion. Today, he's considered one of the fathers of the free love moment and the British equivalent of Alfred Kinsey (more on him later).

It would be wrong to say that Ellis and Sanger enjoyed a *romantic* relationship because that would twist and abuse the concept of romance. In truth, their relationship was strictly sexual. Ellis hardly kept his affair a secret from his poor wife. He wrote detailed, pornographic letters about his escapades with Sanger—and forced his wife to read them. This emotional abuse drove the poor woman, quite literally, out of her mind.[16]

When Ellis wasn't exploring his deviant urges, he was arguing for revolutionary changes in society—and he learned from the best. Ellis was a protégé and disciple of Francis Galton, a scientist whose positive contributions to the world include creating the first weather map and suggesting fingerprints could be used for identification.[17] But Galton was also the father of the modern eugenics movement. In fact, he coined the term *eugenics*.[18] Cobbled together from two Greek roots, *eugenics* means "good birth" and attempts to put a positive spin on a diabolical practice. Galton's philosophies didn't incubate in isolation; he was influenced by his famous cousin Charles Darwin.

Darwin's book *On the Origin of Species by Means of Natural Selection, or the Preservation of Favoured Races in the Struggle for Life* changed the trajectory of the world in a short time. One of the ways it did so was through Galton, who saw in his cousin's book the answer to many of the world's problems. If man is just another animal, however evolved he might be, selective breeding and herd reduction are tools at our disposal. And if "survival of the fittest" is the law of the animal kingdom, who's to say it shouldn't also be the rule in human societies as well?

The book of Genesis provides a Judeo-Christian origin story that clearly delineates man from animals. In fact, according to the Hebrew Scriptures, human beings were crafted in God's image. Human life is precious—all of it, not just those who have certain physical characteristics or meet certain intellectual qualifications. In *The Origin of Species*, however, there is no special creation, no *imago Dei*, and no reason to differentiate humans from baboons. Darwin tells us a different origin story, where the fittest of a species must survive and thrive by any means necessary. Galton latched on to that narrative and introduced the modern eugenics movement to the world as a type of salvation that "the fittest" must secure for themselves. And it's no use talking about right and wrong because in Darwin's world, might is right. Darwin himself had written in 1871, "At some future period, not very distant as measured by centuries, the civilised races of man will almost certainly exterminate and replace throughout the world the savage races."[19] Galton and those who followed after him took this prognostication as a mandate.

To say that Margaret Sanger appreciated Havelock Ellis's work would be an understatement. Dr. George Grant, in his book *Grand Illusions*, describes the relationship between Sanger and Ellis in terms that exceed both their sexual liaisons and their mutual interest in progressive politics:

> To Margaret, Ellis was a modern-day saint. She adored him at once, both for his radical ideas and for his unusual bedroom

behavior. The two of them began to plot a strategy for Margaret's cause. Ellis emphasized the necessity of political expediency. Margaret would have to tone down her pro-abortion stance. She would, he said, have to distance herself from revolutionary rhetoric. The scientific and philanthropic-sounding themes of Malthus and Eugenics would have to replace the politically charged themes of old-line labor Anarchism and Socialism.[20]

We moved quickly from Darwin, to Galton, to Ellis, to Sanger. Within fifty-five years, we moved from the theory that man is an animal (Darwin), to eugenics (Galton), to sexual chaos and perversion being given the veneer of scientific credibility (Ellis), to child sacrifice and the founding of an organization that would murder over twenty million babies in America and many more worldwide. The fact that this ideological thread can be traced through four individuals who taught and mentored one another is more than a little disturbing and proves what I've said for many years: ideas have consequences, and bad ideas have victims.[21]

In late 1915, Sanger returned to the United States and began a public speaking tour. A short time later, the charges she faced for violating federal indecency laws with *The Woman Rebel* were suddenly dropped. Her lectures apparently garnered her sympathy, and with public sentiment in her favor, the federal government's case was closed without a trial.

Not wasting any time, Sanger opened America's first birth control clinic in the Brownsville section of Brooklyn, New York, on October 16, 1916. She was evolving from a rank-and-file activist to a revolutionary pioneer. Like Christ fellowshipping with His Father in the wilderness before beginning His public ministry, Sanger returned from England transformed and immediately got to work. This was no longer theoretical. Sanger's first birth control clinic was a physical unfolding of her new zeal for Darwinism, neo-Malthusianism, sexual revolution, and eugenics. Why didn't Sanger open her illegal clinic in her own neighborhood of Greenwich Village, where many rich, upper-class white folks lived? Because Brownsville was brimming with the very types of people she had a vested interest in targeting. Brownsville was a poor immigrant community comprised of Slavs, Latinos, Italians, and Jews. It was a place inhabited by those she deemed "unfit." Sanger and her sister Ethel were unable to find doctors to help them with their revolutionary, new "contraceptive" procedure, and they illegally performed the procedure themselves.

After just nine days in operation, Sanger was arrested for providing advice about contraceptive techniques. She was later convicted and spent thirty days in jail. She appealed the verdict, and while the court would not overturn the previous decision, it did rule that doctors could prescribe contraceptives to women for medical reasons. Sanger saw this ruling as a loophole that would allow her to continue her work. In 1921, Sanger founded the American Birth Control League, and in 1923, as an initiative of the League, she would open another birth control clinic, this time staffed by a team of female doctors and social workers. These clinics would be the first of many, and the American Birth Control League would later rebrand itself as Planned Parenthood and become one of the best-funded and most profitable non-profit organizations in human history, the largest abortion provider in the world, the pioneer of the radical and obscenely pornographic Comprehensive Sexuality Education (CSE) in much of America's public schools, and as of 2023, the second largest provider of cross-sex hormones and puberty blockers in America. The year 1916 was the beginning of most of the evil now unfolding rapidly across America. For its part, Planned Parenthood has managed to profit from the progressive revolution more than any other organization in the world. The evil they have created and spread has affected every single one of us, whether you know it or not.

Sanger's short stint in prison made her something of a martyr in the eyes of many. She channeled this attention and empathy into her efforts to push eugenics and contraception into mainstream America. She embarked on nationwide lecture tours, preaching the gospel of population control, consequence-free sex, and self-determined morality. And in 1917, Sanger started a new magazine, *The Birth Control Review*. In print, she could reach more people, and she could invite fellow radicals to contribute their ideas. This was the magazine that would later feature the writings of Leon Whitney and many other vile eugenicists.

In the pages of *The Birth Control Review*, readers were greeted with articles arguing for race-based immigration policies, forced sterilization, and the creation of concentration camps on American soil to house undesirables. In 1920, the magazine published a favorable review of Lothrop Stoddard's book *The Rising Tide of Color against White World Supremacy*. Stoddard was a board member of the American Eugenics Society, a high-ranking official in the Massachusetts Ku Klux Klan, and in 1921, became a founding board member for Sanger's American Birth Control League, a position he held for many years.[22] Interestingly, the glowing review was written by Havelock Ellis. And the introduction to Stoddard's racist book was written by Madison Grant. Stoddard also has the distinction of inspiring the Nazi term for non-Aryans, *untermenschen*, literally "undermen" or "subhumans," borrowed from the German edition of another of Stoddard's books, *The Revolt Against Civilization: The Menace of the Under Man*. That's right—the Nazis got their famous untermenschen (subhumans) label from one of Planned Parenthood's first board members. Years later, none other than Heinrich Himmler used the title *Untermenschen* for a book filled with Nazi propaganda.

In 1934, Hans F. Gunther, a German race anthropologist and Nazi intellectual whose work and writings on eugenics won him the Goethe medal for arts and science from Hitler, referred to Lothrop Stoddard and Madison Grant as the "spiritual fathers" of Nazi Germany.[23] Shocking though it may seem, one of Hitler's favorite authors and thinkers referred to the founding board member of Planned Parenthood as the Third Reich's "spiritual father." This love was enduring and reciprocal, it seems, for in 1938, the Nazis invited Stoddard to Berlin to conduct a free-range journalistic interview tour. No American was granted that level of access during the Third Reich. Celebrated author of *The Rise and Fall of The Third Reich*, William Shirer, explains Stoddard's preferential treatment by the Nazis in his published diaries as a journalist in Europe during the 1930s. He complained that the Reich minister for propaganda, Joseph Goebbels, gave special treatment to Lothrop Stoddard because Stoddard's writings on race were "featured in Nazi school textbooks."[24] Stoddard even helped the German Hereditary Supreme Court reach a positive verdict in sterilizing certain Jews.[25] Stoddard met with high-ranking Nazi officials, including Fritz Sauckel, Robert Ley, Hans F. Gunther, and Heinrich Himmler, and even had a brief meeting with Hitler himself. His 1940 book, *Into the Darkness: Nazi Germany Today*, includes an explanation of his meeting with Hitler. It's hard not to blush reading Stoddard's drooling praise of the Führer. Sometime later, a photograph of Stoddard and Hitler taken during their meeting was sent to the American "with the Führer's compliments as a souvenir of the occasion..." but given "with the express understanding that it was not for publication."[26] That's right. One of Planned Parenthood's founding board members is the only American on record to have had a one-on-one meeting with the Führer after he rose to power. Stoddard then gave his full-throated endorsement of Hitler's "solution" and said, "The sterilization law is weeding out the worst strains in the Germanic stock in a scientific and truly humanitarian way."[27] Stoddard had found his hero. At last, here was someone who had coupled his own ideological courage with the political power to enforce that ideology. Published eighteen years before meeting Hitler, Stoddard's very racist book had recommended certain "solutions" to dealing with "bad stock."

> Just as we isolate bacterial invasions and starve out the bacteria by limiting the area and amount of their food-supply, so we can compel an inferior race to remain in its native habitat... [which will] as with all organisms, eventually limit...its influence.[28]

And as with bacteria, the goal in "starving it out" is to eventually eliminate it. Finally, he had found someone who was taking his own "solutions" with a sense of finality; a "final solution."

In 1933, Sanger's *Review* featured an article entitled "Eugenic Sterilization: An Urgent Need" by Ernst Rüdin, a close friend and advisor to Sanger.[29] Among the more shocking statements in this piece, Rüdin recommends a careful propaganda program to mainstream the idea of sterilizing the "unfit." While suggesting that such sterilization "services" should be voluntary, he quickly changed his tune, writing, "There is absolutely no question of using compulsion. Whether in the far future, something of the sort might be required cannot be predicted now."[30] His eugenic "solutions" should not surprise us given that at the time of the article's publication, Rüdin was serving as Adolf Hitler's director of genetic sterilization and had taken a prominent role in the establishment of the Nazi Society for Racial Hygiene.[31] His 1933 article in Sanger's journal was originally published in Germany and was a precursor to the Nazi government's forced-sterilization program, administered by Rüdin himself. That same year, Rüdin also helped craft a sterilization law in Germany, based on US legislation. It was called the Law for the Prevention of Genetically Diseased Offspring and was passed on July 14, 1933.[32] Rüdin was even referred to as "the predominant medical presence in the Nazi sterilization program."[33] During the early 1940s, Rüdin stressed "the value of eliminating young children of inferior quality" and even declared euthanasia to be mere "therapeutic reform."[34] While Rüdin's impact on Nazi "scholarship" and eugenics is hard to overstate, one of his most significant influences was on a young student doctor named Josef Mengele, who regularly attended Rüdin's lectures.[35] Sanger was proud to print Nazi talking points in her magazine. Though she later changed her tone on the Third Reich (after the atrocities committed became public knowledge), she initially championed the "euthanasia, sterilization, abortion, and infanticide programs of the early Reich."[36]

Many of the names in this chapter have been forgotten by all but historians. And yet each one contributed to the culture we experience today. Sanger was right. The sexual revolution had to take hold before there could be a true socialist movement; the church would have to be effectively silenced for deviancy to come out into the light of day. People would need to be desensitized before the culture of death could rise without much of a challenge. We live downstream from Sanger's exploits, but the wickedness she spread in her life was not isolated to a single woman.

There is a straight line from Darwin's evolutionary theory to Sanger's eugenics-laden assault on families and communities and another from American progressives, of which Sanger was one, to the horrors of Auschwitz. Hitler himself once bragged:

> Now that we know the laws of heredity,...it is possible to a large extent to prevent unhealthy and severely handicapped beings from coming into the world. I have studied with interest the laws of several American states concerning prevention of reproduction by people whose progeny would, in all probability, be of no value or be injurious to the racial stock.[37]

The modern progressive movement would not exist if it were not for the unholy trinity of Darwin, Sanger, and Hitler. The first made it fashionable to treat one's neighbor as an animal, the latter showed what that looks like in its most extreme form, and, in the middle, Sanger made the twisted gospel of freedom from God palatable to the point that even men and women who call themselves Christians would willingly lay down their babies on the altar of child sacrifice.

CHAPTER THREE
THE THEOLOGICAL ROOTS OF EVIL

"In a society in which idolatry runs rampant, a church that is not iconoclastic is a travesty. If it is not against the idols it is with them."

—Herbert Schlossberg

Looking back on the socialist movement that spread like wildfire during the first half of the twentieth century, the connections are enough to make a person's head spin. Margaret Sanger is worth our attention because, in America, it's hard to name a figure with more blood on her hands than hers. But she wasn't an anomaly. She was well-seated in her era and had plenty of company in the eugenics crowd. She was no Hitler, but only because she wasn't as popular here as he was in Germany. And even Hitler wouldn't have been who he was if it weren't for Sanger and her ilk.

History is more than connections and anecdotes, of course. And its purpose goes far beyond satisfying curiosities. To discern where we're headed (and what we can do to stop the train), we must reckon with where we've been. But to truly understand what we're up against in our day, we need to take a step further back, to study the picture from a different perspective.

Just a few decades ago, homosexual attraction was considered a mental health problem. A few years ago, the very idea that a man could marry another man (or a woman could marry another woman) was a sick proposition to most Americans. Even in liberal California, when put to a vote, same-sex marriage was denied legal status.[1] Now, we live in a culture where biological men compete on female sports teams and use the ladies' room, where elementary school teachers educate students on changing their gender identity, and school libraries are stocked with books about gender transitions and oral sex. "The 1619 Project" is helping make sure this emerging generation hates America, and Wall Street is using its leverage to make sure businesses across this land are more focused on skin color than on performance. And that's just the stuff we've gotten used to seeing nightly on cable news. Meanwhile, out in California, a bellwether state for American culture's direction:

- The state is attempting to define an LGBT couple's inability to reproduce as "infertility." This would give such couples insurance-paid access to fertility treatments, including artificial insemination of pregnancy surrogates. In other words, a man will acquire the "right" to a woman's uterus and the ability to purchase children through surrogacy. This is all being done in the name of so-called fertility inequality.[2]
- As of this writing, there is a bill making its way through the legislative process that would allow twelve-year-old children to pump themselves full of chemical-castration drugs and have their genitals lopped off without a parent's consent if "professionals" feel it would be harmful to inform the parents.[3]
- Another bill would allow the state to take gender-confused minors from their parents if the parents refused to use their preferred pronouns and didn't support their "transitions."[4]

- Yet another bill on the table would require sex education instructors to teach students how and where to obtain an abortion.[5]
- There's even a proposed law that would enable activists to sue pro-life pregnancy centers and churches that share false or misleading information on abortion.[6] I'm sure you can imagine just who would get to define what is "false" or "misleading." The result of such a law would be to further silence the church in California from speaking out against the ceaseless murder of the unborn.

It's hard to categorize what we see happening in our society. We're so far afield from traditional conservative-versus-liberal debates. This goes beyond Republican or Democrat. It's not even political. In fact, calling the current culture war a political debate only masks the danger we're facing. Political cycles come and go, but the stakes here require new categories.

Journalist Tucker Carlson, not known for religious sophistry, sentimentalism, or superstition, stumbled into this mystery the weekend before his well-known dismissal from Fox News. Speaking at The Heritage Foundation, the institution where he began his career in the early 1990s, Carlson reflected on our cultural moment with uncommon insight:

> Policy papers don't account for it at all. If you have people who are saying, "I have an idea. Let's castrate the next generation. Let's sexually mutilate children"—I'm sorry. That's not a political debate. That has nothing to do with politics. What's the outcome we're desiring here? An androgynous population? Is that really what we are arguing for? No, I don't think anyone could, like, defend that as a positive outcome. But the weight of the government and—you know—a lot of corporate interests are behind that.... It's irrational.
>
> If you say, "Well, you know, I think abortion is always bad," [and someone else says,] "Well, I think sometimes it's neces-

sary," that's a debate I'm familiar with. But if you're telling me that abortion is a positive good, what are you saying? Well, you're arguing for child sacrifice.... When the treasury secretary stands up and says, "You know what you can do to help the economy? Get an abortion," well, that's like an Aztec principle.

None of this makes sense in conventional political terms. When people or crowds of people—or the largest crowd of people of all, which is the federal government, the largest human organization in human history—decide that the goal is to destroy things...what you're watching is not a political movement. It's evil.... I'm not calling for a religious war—far from it—I'm merely calling for an acknowledgment of what we're watching.[7]

Evil. It's a strong word and one that should never be tossed out lightly. It's a term that sums up opposition to God, first and foremost. And because God is the greatest champion of human flourishing, that which is evil seeks to destroy all that is good and beneficial for humanity. Tucker Carlson is right. It's difficult to make the case that what we're seeing right now in our country—and the larger world—can be explained with political theory. There is something deeper at work, something most ivory-tower academics and cable news pundits cannot see. Even if they could, they'd never admit it.

But Margaret Sanger would. Here's what she wrote in an issue of *The Woman Rebel*, "Birth control appeals to the advanced radical because it is calculated to undermine the authority of the Christian churches. I look forward to seeing humanity free someday of the tyranny of Christianity no less than Capitalism."[8] Her mission was religious, and she admitted it without hesitation. She wanted to see the church of Jesus Christ undone.

In the late nineteenth century, Cardinal Henry Edward Manning said something profound—so profound that it's been repeated, reiterated, and (at times) stolen ever since: "All human conflict is ultimately theological." At first, the statement seems preposterous. Of course, conflicts have been waged on other grounds, we assume. But the more we sit with Manning's words, the more we come to find they are indeed true.

Reflecting on the words of Cardinal Manning years later, writer and historian Hilaire Belloc wrote:

> This saying of his (which I carried away with me somewhat bewildered) "that all human conflict is ultimately theological": that is, that all wars and revolutions and all decisive struggles between parties of men arise from a difference in morals and Transcendental doctrine, was utterly novel to me. To a young man the saying was without meaning: I would have almost said nonsensical, save that I could not attach the idea of folly to Manning. But as I grew older it became a searchlight: with the observation of the world, and with continuous reading of history, it came to possess for me a universal meaning so profound that it reached to the very roots of political action; so extended that it covered the whole.[9]

In truth, Manning wasn't the first one to notice this phenomenon. In the ancient world, it was inescapable. It is only in our post-Enlightenment era, when men consider themselves beyond the reach of the gods, that such a statement is even noteworthy. But here we are, having to remember a truth so ingrained in our DNA as human beings that when we do recognize it, it will seem so very obvious.

Theology, done right, always takes the form of a story. God did not give us a book of propositions; rather, He gave us a story. It begins with the Bible, the single most important book ever written, and it's a story you and I now find ourselves in. But to know our part, we must understand where we've been. To do that, we must go back to the very beginning...

There's something wrong with this world. Everyone feels it. Not a soul can deny it. Somehow, we all know that pain and suffering do not belong, and neither does death, sickness, loneliness, or heartache. They are corruptions, invasive species infecting an otherwise good world. But how do we explain it? As we've already seen, Darwin posited that death and suffering are standard features of nature, that they're the tools of evolution leading us closer and closer to utopia. But the Bible tells a different story.

Scripture confirms what we already know inherently: we were made for a different sort of world—one without death, pain, or loneliness. And that is precisely the kind of world God gave to us. "It was very good" (Genesis 1:31b). Not only was life in the garden of Eden free from pain and filled with joy; it was life in God's presence. Human beings were made for God—to be part of His family. That is why the Gospel of Jesus Christ is good news; it's our invitation back home. But I'm getting ahead of myself.

Paradise was lost when our first parents, Adam and Eve, listened to the evil one instead of to God. They believed the lie that God was holding out on them, and they ate the forbidden fruit. In that moment, the world was forever changed. Sin entered in and held the door open for suffering and death. Adam and Eve were sent into exile, and they lost their place in God's family.

If you've ever been to Sunday school, that much you know. But here's the bit that's pertinent to our discussion: ever since Adam and Eve walked out of the garden, humanity has been attempting to find a way back in. God promised to send a Savior. He told Adam and Eve a child would be born who would crush the head of the serpent who deceived them. The promised one would destroy evil and set things right. But we human beings are stubborn in our sin; we want a way back home on our own terms—without God.

The first major offensive to get back into the garden is recorded in Genesis 11. There, people settled on a plain in Shinar. Settling down was itself an act of rebellion, for God had commanded the human race to "fill the earth and subdue it" (Genesis 1:28b). But the greater rebellion was the tower they attempted to build:

> They said to each other, "Come, let's make bricks and bake them thoroughly." They used brick instead of stone, and tar

for mortar. Then they said, "Come, let us build ourselves a city, with a tower that reaches to the heavens, so that we may make a name for ourselves; otherwise we will be scattered over the face of the whole earth." (Genesis 11:3–4)

Calling it a "tower that reaches to the heavens" wasn't just another way of saying, "It will be really, really tall!" It was instead a theological statement:

The tower of Babel is regarded by all scholars as one of Mesopotamia's famous man-made sacred mountains—a ziggurat. Ziggurats were divine abodes, places where Mesopotamians believed heaven and earth intersected. The nature of this structure makes evident the purpose in building it—to bring the divine down to earth.[10]

Atop the tower of Babel would have been a temple—a place where human beings could mingle with the gods. Eden had been a place where heaven met earth; that is why God dwelled there with His people. Babel was an attempt to recreate Eden, to get back home.

While there's nothing wrong with having a desire for Eden—in fact, that desire is part of our humanity—the wicked people who gathered in Shinar were attempting to recreate Paradise on their own terms, apart from God. They wanted utopia without salvation, heaven without redemption, and a way back home without the Father. You may have wondered why God came down and confused the language of the people so the building would have to stop. If they were just building a run-of-the-mill ancient skyscraper, His response would have been overkill. But they were trying to save themselves, and in doing so, condemning humanity to a life apart from God.

Babel wasn't the last attempt to build a stairway to heaven. History is filled with examples. Socialism's promise of utopia is, in many ways, Babel by another name. Collectivism and government control are the bricks used. In every case, the goal is a better society, free from [insert problem here], and the paradise promised is always engineered apart from God. For Karl Marx, paradise was a world where classes were abolished and the government held centralized power to dispense daily bread. The Nazis promised a beautiful, vibrant, expanded German Reich with no poverty or disease. And Herbert Marcuse, one of the leading neo-Marxists of the sexual revolution, spoke for the entire movement when, in his creepy 1955 sex book, *Eros and Civilization*, he said for man to be redeemed, "the 'original sin' must be committed again: 'We must again eat from the tree of knowledge in order to fall back into the state of innocence.'"[11] Interestingly, Marcuse was one of the most significant members and teachers of the Frankfurt School and was a mentor to Angela Davis, who, as mentioned previously, directly mentored the co-founders of BLM Inc. Is it starting to make sense?

Sanger was on board with Marcuse's sentiments decades earlier. For her, utopia was a society free from repressive morality and religious superstition, where sex was unleashed and permissible in any and every permutation. Here's Sanger in her own words: "Through sex, mankind may attain the great spiritual illumination which will transform the world, which will light up the only path to an earthly paradise."[12] Sex was a path back to Eden. Sanger's life's work was a vain attempt to build a tower to heaven, to achieve salvation without a Savior.

―――

There's another element of the quest for Eden borrowed from the ancient world—child sacrifice. The book of 2 Kings records an episode in which Joram, the king of Israel, and Jehoshaphat, the king of Judah, went up to fight against Mesha, the king of Moab. Israel and Judah's forces were winning the field, and it seemed like the battle would be theirs. But then, something happened:

> When the king of Moab saw that the battle had gone against him, he took with him seven hundred swordsmen to break through to the king of Edom, but they failed. Then he took his firstborn son, who was to succeed him as king, and offered him as a sacrifice on the city wall. The fury against Israel was great;

they withdrew and returned to their own land. (2 Kings 3:26–27)

This scene serves as but one example of an ancient practice, not only kept in the Middle East but throughout the world. People would sacrifice their children to the gods in exchange for peace and prosperity. They understood there was more to the cosmos than what they could see with their eyes, so to please the gods they believed held sway over their lives, they gave them what was most precious to them to demonstrate their loyalty and receive blessings.

Why did the gods demand child sacrifices? These demons are evil, and as we've already discussed, evil is opposed to God and human flourishing. Every child bears God's image, and everyone is a gift from God, a blessing for our good. So, of course, evil wants children to die. God brings life, and evil can only bring death. As my godfather Gregg Cunningham says, "Satan would kill God if he could, but he can't. So, he kills babies because he knows it wounds the heart of God."

The devil has always had a vested interest in destroying children. Back in Genesis 3:15, God had promised that one born of a woman would crush the serpent. Two thousand years ago, that baby arrived, and His name was Jesus of Nazareth. Even so, human beings are an incessant reminder to the enemy of our souls that his days are numbered. There is a day coming when he will be thrown into the lake of fire. So, in the meantime, he will cause as much chaos and heartache as he can manage. Concerning the ancient pagan view of children, Rabbi Jonathan Cahn writes:

> Even children born perfectly healthy could be murdered if, for some reason, they were not found desirable or wanted by their parents. And even some of the most revered philosophers and esteemed leaders of the ancient world could endorse or decree the death of innocent children. It was not safe to be a child in the ancient pagan world. One could be murdered at the moment of one's birth, or before or after. It was not at all uncommon for children to be killed in their mother's wombs.

With the pagan devaluation of human life came a bent toward death—the spirit of Molech.[13]

You may recall that in Genesis 22, God told Abraham to sacrifice Isaac in the mountains of Moriah. Abraham didn't question the command but was diligent in obeying. Why? Because it was a common practice for worshipers of ancient gods to sacrifice their children. Of course, God was only testing Abraham, and He intervened with a substitute—a ram that foreshadowed the ultimate substitute, Jesus. One of the reasons Christianity is revolutionary is that, in Christianity, God does not demand our children be sacrificed; rather, He gave *His* Son to secure our peace and prosperity. Abortion says, "You must die so I can live." But Christ says, "No, I must die so you can live."

The idea of child sacrifice may seem ridiculous to us today, but it's still happening. It is worth repeating what Tucker Carlson said: "If you're telling me that abortion is a positive good, what are you saying? Well, you're arguing for child sacrifice.... When the treasury secretary stands up and says, 'You know what you can do to help the economy? Get an abortion,' well, that's like an Aztec principle."[14]

Rabbi Cahn sees the devaluing of human life as an unavoidable element once a society turns to a worldview grounded in anything other than the Bible:

> When a nation or civilization turns away from God, we can expect the same values and horrors to be revived. It is no accident that the same nation that turned from Christian faith and replaced biblical values with pagan ones, Nazi Germany, came to view the sickly and weak as contemptible and disposable, then set out to exterminate them. So too when the Soviet government purged biblical values from Russia, human life, likewise, became disposable. In each case, the departure from biblical values to pagan or neo-pagan values resulted in the murder of millions.[15]

Of course, it's not just the Nazis and the Soviets who came to view human life as expendable. Abortion clinics dot the landscape of the United States as a testament to our culture's shift away from biblical values in our scramble toward paganism. Nazis from the 1930s and abortionists today might not refer to their acts as child sacrifices to the gods, but that's what it is. It's only that, in the modern era, the dark gods are less obvious than they were in the ancient world. However, their influence is still the same:

> Bloodthirsty gods produce bloodthirsty people. If someone thinks that chance rules the universe, his actions are likely to appear random. If people increasingly think that malevolence rules…we can expect more human sacrifice. If there is a decline in the number of people who believe that God is love, we can expect fewer who think that actions of love are moral imperatives. For any individual or society, therefore, the religious questions are the ultimate ones that govern human conduct, whether they believe it or not.[16]

Even in something that was once thought to be benign—environmentalism—we can see the bloodlust of the gods. Today's environmental movement is quite different from previous generations' attempts to keep pollution in check and preserve the planet's natural resources. Now, Mother Gaia is worshiped as a god, and the devil in this story is humanity. We are the problem, and the only solution is to retreat. We must stop making any impact on the environment—no fossil fuels, no infrastructure, no deforestation. We must learn to live in the background of an undisturbed natural world, and the best thing we can do for the goddess is simply to die. We must return the world to its pre-industrial status when 90 percent of the population lived in poverty.[17] And, of course, we must abort the next generation because more humans on this planet will only hurt poor Mother Earth. Gone are the days of saying we must preserve the planet for our kids and grandkids. Today, it's best not to have children at all.

In a 2019 town hall on climate change, Senator Bernie Sanders said he thought the US should provide funding for abortion and contraceptives to combat climate change. As if that weren't shocking enough, Sanders said the US government should send this funding *to poor countries*. This wasn't a town hall about abortion. It was supposed to be about caring for the environment and fighting a supposedly looming climate catastrophe, yet Bernie went full-on, "We must appease the sun god!" I hope you can sense the demonic hysteria that's in operation here.

In her book, *The Sacrament of Abortion* (yes, that's really the title), psychologist Ginette Paris wrote:

> I have drawn inspiration throughout this book from a guiding image, the Artemis of Greek mythology [the goddess of childbirth]... It is not immoral to choose abortion; it is simply another kind of morality, a pagan one. It is time to stop being defensive about it, time to point an accusatory finger at the other camp and denounce its own immoral stance. Abortion is a sacrifice to Artemis. Abortion is a sacrament for the gift of life to remain pure. Our culture needs new rituals as well as laws to restore abortion to its sacred dimension, which is both terrible and necessary.

As if in response to Paris's twisted assertion, Peter Kreeft wrote, "Abortion is the demonic parody of the Eucharist. That's why it uses the same holy words. This is my body. But with the opposite blasphemous meaning." It is a reversal of God's sacrifice for man—a woman's sacrifice for demons. It doesn't get more evil than that. Rather than accepting the broken body and the shed blood of Christ for eternal life, the culture of death demands that we break the bodies and shed the blood of babies for eternal life. Sound hyperbolic? Just wait. Ever heard of embryonic stem cell research? How about fetal organ harvesting and fetal tissue research? What about prenatal gene editing? What's the common denominator? The baby is sacrificed in man's pursuit of eternal life. The baby is traded for the fountain of pharmaceutical youth. Christ says, "This is my body and I break it for you." Abortion says, "This is my body and I break you baby, for me." It's not a coincidence that the central phrase of the entire abortion industrial complex and the broader sexualized culture is, "This is my body!" So, if I want to murder the fruit of my womb or mutilate my genitals, it's my choice! It should therefore come as no surprise that Planned Parenthood makes "bodily autonomy" arguments for both abortion and transgender surgeries. And they call both mutilating acts "healthcare." Abortion becomes "reproductive healthcare," and transgender "eunuch" surgery becomes "gender-affirming healthcare."

There's yet another ancient thread of evil that has made its way into our modern era unchecked: Gnosticism. The heresy of Gnosticism plagued the early church, insisting on a dualistic view of the universe. In Gnostic theology, it was believed the material world was created accidentally and through evil intent by a demigod, a being willfully ignorant of the good and true God. The only way to triumph over this evil world is by obtaining secret knowledge.[18]

This theology means everything material is warped, untrue, and cannot be trusted. It is inferior to the spiritual world. That which is physical can be disregarded and even severed from its connection to the metaphysical and spiritual. Physical realities, then, are not a reality at all but can be redefined and shaped to fit the preferences of an individual.

Also called the materialist view, this belief system holds that nature is a product of blind, material forces; the body is just a shell of skin, bones, and organs; and the mind is essentially a playground to be used however a person desires. The mind is the place of actual identity. You are your mind. Of course, if the materialist view of the world were true, we would have no way to be certain, since the mind itself is subject to one's whims and preferences. C. S. Lewis put it this way, "Unless I believe in God, I cannot believe in thought: so I can never use thought to disbelieve in God."[19]

The early church rightly saw Gnosticism as a dangerous heresy, for God created everything—both material and immaterial, physical and spiritual. God declared the physical world "very good" (Genesis 1:31), and even sent His Son to earth to be born of a virgin. Jesus took on a human body, and though that body was transformed at His resurrection, He never took off His flesh. He is still fully divine *and* fully human. To suggest that the physical is inferior to the spiritual is to divide God's creation where it should not be, and it's to deny the gospel, which declares salvation can only be found in the God who became man. As author and Christian apologist Nancy Pearcey beautifully explains:

> What really set Christianity apart in the ancient world, however, was the incarnation—the claim that the most High God had himself entered into the realm of matter, taking on a physical body. In Gnosticism, the highest deity would have nothing to do with the material world.[20]

It's all well and good to discuss Gnosticism as an ancient curiosity, but it didn't get buried in the ash heap of history as an alternative theology that was ultimately set aside. Gnosticism is still with us today; it just goes by other names.

In Gnosticism, the mind is the connection point to the spiritual realm, so it is the key to a fulfilled life. With so-called "secret knowledge," Gnostics hope to achieve a spiritual enlightenment that will take them into truth. In true Gnostic fashion (though he wouldn't have called it that), René Descartes said, "I think, therefore I am." Notice that he places the "authentic human identity in the mind alone. The implication is that the body is not an aspect of the true self; instead the body is a mechanism that serves the needs and desires of the mind, like the pilot of a ship or the driver of a car."[21] Philosopher Daniel Dennett says, "Since Descartes in the seventeenth century we have had a vision of the self as a sort of immaterial ghost that owns and controls a body, the way you own and control your car."[22] Is it any wonder that today there are people who want to take their "car" into a "body shop" and give it a "makeover" that reflects the "real" person on the inside? Transgenderism asserts that people have a right to make the outside look how the inside feels.

We see this same Gnostic dualism when it comes to abortion—the child growing inside a mother's womb is human but not yet a *person*. This is contrary to the truth the material world gives us—but since dualists discount truth gained from the observation of nature, they cannot accept it. Australian philosopher and professor of bioethics Peter Singer writes:

> It is possible to give "human being" a precise meaning. We can use it as the equivalent to "member of the species homo sapiens." Whether a being is a member of a given species is something that can be determined scientifically, by an examination of the nature of the chromosomes in the cells of living organisms. In this sense, there is no doubt that from the first moments of its existence an embryo conceived from human sperm and eggs is a human being.[23]

And yet, this same Peter Singer is infamous for his support for the infanticide of babies up to one year old. Why? Because the qualities that allegedly ground *personhood*, which are absent in the unborn, continue to remain absent in the newborn. This is why an unborn baby can be considered a human but not a person by many progressives. While most of us continue to use the words *human* and *person* synonymously, these two terms were ripped apart by the Supreme Court in 1973. In *Roe v. Wade*, there was no disputing the unborn child was fully human, but he was deemed a "non-person" without dignity or rights.

Understand this: Since Gnostics and their intellectual descendants believe real human identity is found in the mind—the realm of thoughts, aims, consciousness, and desires—the baby in the womb is not yet a person because he or she is not yet developmentally advanced enough to have desires. When an abortionist kills a baby in his mother's womb, she doesn't kill a person; she merely dissects a body. Who, then, decides when a human being is a person? The state.

Pearcey explains:

> The only way the state can legalize abortion is to deny the relevance of biology and declare that some biological humans are not persons. The state has taken on itself the authority to decide which humans qualify for the status of personhood,

defined in terms of mental abilities—the capacity to think, feel, and desire. The same reasoning is being applied to euthanasia and assisted suicide as well.[24]

Are you seeing how religious all of this is? For a movement that wants to push Christianity out of the public square, its adherents are themselves fundamentally religious in every way that matters. The belief system undergirding their policies and the issues they champion are all held together by faith.

Man is fundamentally a religious being. Being created by God as an eternal being, we cannot help but live as religious people. And the more humanity tries to advance beyond religion, the more we begin to resemble adherents of every weird and kooky religion that has come before us. Strip Christianity from a society and we go right back to demon worship. Or to quote my earthly hero, Pastor Jack Hibbs, "Sacrificing babies is what man does without God."[25] Is it surprising, then, that when Cory Booker was running for the Democratic nomination for president, he declared abortion "one of the most sacrosanct ideals in our country?"[26] You might be tempted to believe it was just a poor choice of words, but *sacrosanct* means "most sacred or holy, inviolable."[27] What was once only said in private is now being declared publicly.

These three strands of ancient religion that feed into today's Marxism-infused progressive revolution—striving for Eden without God, child sacrifice, and Gnosticism—are not alone. Other elements manifest, but these are at the core of radical Leftism, a truly religious movement being unleashed in a way that the world has never seen. All three strands bring death, so we shouldn't be surprised to find that in places where these ideas are put into practice, death follows.

What is needed in this theological war are men and women who will stand on the side of truth, who will speak up and condemn these diabolical ideas before they are allowed to spread further. Dietrich Bonhoeffer tried in his day. He is known to us today as a man who stood up in his native Germany and spoke out against the evils of the Nazi regime—and he paid for his boldness with his life. But he was just one pastor among a few thousand willing to speak. The vast majority of Lutheran clergy in Germany were silent—and some even supported Hitler.

> Before the Nazis could murder the actual Christian Church, the aforementioned Christian leaders in 1934 drafted and published what has come be called the Barmen Declaration. It essentially said that the German state must not and could not co-opt the Church, that the sanctity and separation of the Church from the state must be clear....
>
> But what is shocking to us today is that most pastors in Germany were not willing to sign it. Either they were not thinking clearly on the subject at hand, and as a result were not thinking biblically, or perhaps they were thinking clearly enough, but they simply did not have the courage to act on what they knew to be true.[28]

We are in a religious war. It's not being fought with guns and tanks, but it is very real. Now is the time to stand up and speak. Now is the time to be counted, even if it costs us something. Just as it was in Bonhoeffer's day, this is what's being asked of the church. In 1930s Germany, the church failed. Just 3,000 of the approximately 18,000 pastors in the nation were willing to sign the Barmen Declaration. Another 3,000 supported the Nazi regime. But 12,000 were silent![29]

Imagine if those 12,000 pastors had taken a stand with the 3,000. What a difference it would have made in Germany! Bonhoeffer knew the church was not there to simply "bandage the victims under the wheel, but to jam a spoke in the wheel itself."[30] In other words, Christians cannot stay downstream from culture, content to help progressivism's victims put back the pieces of their lives. Instead, we must face the lies head-on—to save the victims before they're trampled.

Sadly, the situation in the United States today is eerily similar to the one in 1930s Germany. While some believers are standing up to the forces of evil that are threatening the lives of the unborn, the sanctity of the family, and the influence of the church, many more are not. They either don't want to ruffle any feathers or they agree with the agenda of radical progressives—they've fooled themselves into thinking the teachings of Jesus Christ are somehow compatible with Critical Race Theory, transgenderism, and abortion on demand.

We all know how things turned out for Germany. Millions died, and the nation was shattered. The long trail of suffering can still be seen today. I'm sad to say, the stakes are even higher in our time. For far too long, the church in America has gotten by with comfortable church services and feel-good sermons, not wanting to get political or offend visitors. But it's time to wake up.

In Paul's letter to the church at Ephesus, he writes:

> Put on the full armor of God, so that you can take your stand against the devil's schemes. For our struggle is not against flesh and blood, but against the rulers, against the authorities, against the powers of this dark world and against the spiritual forces of evil in the heavenly realms. (Ephesians 6:11–12)

We are in a spiritual war, the root of which can be found in ideas. Just look around—ideas have consequences, and we are seeing the impact of very bad ideas. The theology that is driving our culture is from, as Paul puts it, "the spiritual forces of evil in the heavenly realms" (v. 12). Our participation in the battle is not optional. The only question is, which side will we be on? Will we stand firm in the truth, speaking out and refusing to submit, or will we be silent and inconspicuous, tacitly giving aid and comfort to the enemy? That is the choice set before us. And each day we must choose.

CHAPTER FOUR
1916 AND THE RACE TO DESTROY THE "UNFIT"

"If Darwinism was the doctrine of the survival of the fittest, then eugenics was the doctrine of the survival of the nastiest."

—G. K. Chesterton

"So, how did we get here?" That's the question a lot of people are asking today. They look around, and the world no longer seems familiar. Nothing is as it was just a few decades ago. Our society has changed so radically, so quickly, they don't how to account for it. But that's the thing about looking back and attempting to retrace steps—no one does it until they realize they're lost.

If you were to pull on a thread and let the fabric unravel, I believe it would lead you back to October 16, 1916. That's the date when everything changed. Of course, at the time, no one really knew what had happened. No one could feel it. There was nothing in the newspaper headlines, and few people were talking about it. But something happened on that fall day that changed the world. Margaret Sanger opened one of the first birth control clinics in the country—and the very first one in New York.

It was an act of further defiance from a woman who had already faced legal trouble for disseminating information about contraceptives and family planning. It was an outpost of death planted within a culture that did not yet understand where progressivism would lead. The horrors of Nazi Germany were still decades away. But Margaret Sanger was a true believer—not just in feminism or in the supposed right of a woman to kill her unborn child but in the sexual revolution, eugenics, and the culture of death. And in 1916, she took a decisive step toward leaving a legacy that would forever change the world.

If you want to understand how we got to third-trimester abortions, infanticide, euthanasia, pornographic sex-ed, critical race theory, transgenderism, trans-ing children, drag-queen-story-hour for children, arresting pro-life sidewalk counselors, and labeling parents who speak at school board meetings as "domestic terrorists," you have to go back to 1916 when Sanger opened her first illegal birth control clinic in the Brownsville section of New York, an area heavily populated by those she deemed "unfit" to reproduce. The real systemic racism, the real systematic bigotry, the real culture of death is the one architected by the very revolutionaries behind "The 1619 Project" and the Leviathan that mainstreams their lies. The sinister spirit of 1916 has swept through every nook and cranny of American culture, with no area of society left untouched. Therefore, every aspect of our current culture can be viewed and understood in one way or another through the lens of 1916.

In truth, we could go back further to identify the roots of Sanger's twisted philosophy, or we could pinpoint events that came later that had a decisive impact on our culture. But 1916 is the year when Sanger's demonic faith became sight and her ideas began to have real-world consequences. That small clinic in Brownsville, which was only open less than two weeks, was the embodiment of a darkness we can still feel today.

In this chapter and the next, we will look at two streams of evil flowing from 1916. First, we'll examine the racist, eugenics-laden spirit of death that Sanger championed, which the Nazis borrowed, and is now ingrained in our culture. Then, we'll turn our attention toward the sexual revolution in all its perverted and subversive darkness, and how this freedom to debase and dehumanize ourselves and one

1916 AND THE RACE TO DESTROY THE "UNFIT"

another is connected to Sanger's sexual proclivities. But first, let's explore 1916 as the pivotal year in which our country turned its trajectory toward division and death.

If we were looking merely to trace the history of abortion in this country, 1916 would be a good destination. It would be hard to argue that the first brick-and-mortar birth control clinic wasn't a major step toward abortion on demand as it exists in many states today, which was until the summer of 2022 the law of the land. When we think back to the Center for Medical Progress videos of Planned Parenthood employees talking callously about the dismembering and sale of baby body parts, it's difficult not to recognize Sanger's Brownsville location as the starting point. Of course, Margaret Sanger, as the founder of Planned Parenthood, is central to the blood-stained story of abortion on American shores and beyond. But there's more that emanated from that first birth control clinic in New York City.

For starters, Sanger could have planted her flag anywhere in New York City. She could have established her pilot birth control clinic in her own neighborhood of Greenwich Village. But she didn't. She intentionally set up shop at 46 Amboy Street in the Brownsville section of the city, a working-class section of Brooklyn that was home to a diverse population. Today, you may hear apologists for Sanger who argue that the location was chosen to help the working-class poor. As Dr. George Grant rightly pointed out, "The truth is, Planned Parenthood appears to want to *eliminate* the poor, not *serve* them."[1] This is true in our day, and it was true in the beginning with that first Brownsville Clinic.

Don't believe me? Just read Sanger's magazine, where she served as editor-in-chief. In a 1919 editorial, just three years after Brownsville, we find the true purpose of birth control, "More children from the fit, less from the unfit.... That is the chief issue of birth control."[2] That's why she chose Brownsville—to target the "unfit" she believed were dragging down society as a whole. And like all rotten eugenicist thinkers, Sanger also really didn't like people with physical and mental disabilities. Allowing them to have children would be an injustice as far as she was concerned. In one of her more shocking articles entitled, "The Eugenic Value of Birth Control Propaganda," she wrote that "the most urgent problem today is how to limit and discourage the over-fertility of the mentally and physically defective."[3]

For Sanger, birth control was not a tool to lift up the poor and help them "plan" their "parenthood." Far from it. Birth control was merely a weapon in the eugenicists' arsenal to "segregate" and "sterilize" the "choking human undergrowth" of "morons" and "imbeciles."[4] So closely knit were the aims of the eugenics movement and the "birth control" movement that Sanger could only use biblical analogies to explain their relationship. Speaking of her 1923 Birth Control Conference, she told a colleague, "I believe that this conference is going to do much to unite the Eugenic Movement and the Birth Control movement, for after all they should be and are the right and left hand of one body."[5] Borrowing directly from one of Jesus's parables, Sanger wrote, "Eugenics without Birth Control seems to us a house built upon the sands. It is at the mercy of the *rising stream* of the unfit."[6] In other words, Sanger was trying to build a house called eugenics, but if that house was built without birth control, it would be like a house built on sand, so if the "rain came down, the streams rose, and the winds blew and beat against that house," it would "fall with a great crash."[7] Accordingly, if you built the house called eugenics *with* birth control, then if the "rain came down, the streams rose, and the winds blew and beat against that house," it would "not fall because it had its foundation on the rock."[8]

Finally, in an admission that still causes Planned Parenthood to blush and attempt to explain away their founder's virulent racism,[9] Sanger defined what birth control really meant to her. In 1923, Sanger wrote in *The New York Times*:

> Birth Control is not contraception indiscriminately and thoughtlessly practiced. It means the release and cultivation of the better racial elements in our society, and the gradual suppression, elimination and eventual extinction of defective

stocks—those human weeds which threaten the blooming of the finest flowers of American civilization.[10]

Sanger was a eugenicist through and through, and she hardly kept that fact a secret. Of course, before World War II, she didn't have to. These ideas were popular among progressives in the United States. Progressives proudly spoke of work farms for the alcohol-addicted, the unemployable, and the chronically ill. If someone were to say to you, "Follow the science" back then, it meant following the logic of forced sterilization. From Harvard to Princeton to Nobel Prize-winning scientists to the Museum of Natural History, eugenics was seen as the obvious next step in human development. Society needed to be freed from the shackles of the poor, the weak, the ill, and especially those races that did not produce the sort of people who moved the world forward.

In 1924, the Commonwealth of Virginia passed a law entitled the Eugenical Sterilization Act, which allowed doctors to forcibly sterilize "the feeble-minded." There were restrictions, of course. The person had to already be in a mental health facility, and a hearing had to take place. But the result was that the commonwealth had the power to sterilize people deemed "unfit". In 1927, a court case revolving around the issue of forced sterilization made it to the US Supreme Court. Carrie Buck was a young woman whose adoptive family had her committed to the Virginia State Colony for Epileptics and Feebleminded. The superintendent of the home, Dr. John Priddy, wanted Buck sterilized, and a court case ensued. Priddy was eventually succeeded by John Hendren Bell, and in 1927 *Buck v. Bell* made its way to the US Supreme Court.

So powerful were the ideas surrounding eugenics that the Virginia law was upheld by our nation's highest court in an eight-to-one decision. In fact, in the majority opinion, Oliver Wendell Holmes wrote, quite bluntly, "Three generations of imbeciles are enough."[11] The Virginia sterilization law was not the last attempt to legalize the principles of eugenics. Many other states passed similar laws. It is believed that as many as 70,000 Americans were forcibly sterilized in the aftermath of *Buck v. Bell*.[12] At the time, Margaret Sanger supported and celebrated the Court's decision, though again, she was not an extremist to do so.[13] Eugenics and forced sterilization were mainstream. Uncomfortable though it may be to acknowledge, America's eugenics movement and its leaders provided the inspiration and playbook for Hitler's eugenic policies in the Third Reich. In 1934, while Germany was sterilizing more than 5,000 people per month, California eugenics leader C. M. Goethe returned from Germany and bragged to a colleague:

> You will be interested to know that your work has played a powerful part in shaping the opinions of the group of intellectuals who are behind Hitler in this epoch-making program. Everywhere I sensed that their opinions have been tremendously stimulated by American thought…I want you, my dear friend, to carry this thought with you for the rest of your life, that you have really jolted into action a great government of 60 million people.[14]

The same year, Joseph DeJarnette, the superintendent of Virginia's Western State Hospital complained in the *Richmond Times-Dispatch*, "The Germans are beating us at our own game."[15] But perhaps the impact of *Buck v. Bell* on Hitler's policies is best illustrated in this: at the Nuremberg Trials, the Nazis cited our Supreme Court decision, *Buck v. Bell* in their defense, as if to say, "We just copied you."

Five years after the atrocious decision, Sanger defended the horrific injustice that *Buck v. Bell* had unleashed, writing, "Apply a stern and rigid policy of sterilization and segregation to that grade of population whose progeny is tainted, or whose inheritance is already such that objectionable traits may be transmitted to offspring."[16] Hillary Clinton put her own spin on Sanger's eugenicism when, in 2016, she referred to the "deplorables" and "irredeemables." Lest you accuse me of sensationalism, fast-forward to October of 2023 when Hillary Clinton told CNN in an interview that we need to consider "formal deprogramming" of Trump supporters.[17]

In 1925, Sanger hosted the International Neo-Malthusian and

Birth Control Conference at the Hotel McAlpin in New York City. There, she said the following:

> The government of the United States deliberately encourages and even makes necessary by its laws the breeding—with a breakneck rapidity—of idiots, defectives, diseased, feeble-minded, and criminal classes. Billions of dollars are expensed by our state and federal governments and by private charities and philanthropies for the care, the maintenance, and the perpetuation of these classes. Year by year more money is expensed...to maintain an increasing race of morons which threatens the very foundations of our civilization.[18]

Sanger's penchant for destroying lives through sterilization is alive and well today. With the trans movement in full swing, millions of confused, deeply troubled, and psychologically ill individuals are lining up to be mutilated by unnecessary *Frankenstein* surgeries and forever altered mentally and hormonally via pharmaceutical experiments that provide no path to well-being. The result is a generation that is sterilizing itself as the Left cheers on, waving the so-called equality flag high and denouncing anyone who objects as a hate-filled bigot.

In recent years, Planned Parenthood's revenue stream has shifted and grown as a result of this trend that they helped stoke through their perverse sexual education curriculum. The transgender industry is now Planned Parenthood's fastest-growing revenue stream, which includes cross-sex hormones, puberty blockers, literature, curricula, conferences for educators and medical practitioners, government contracts, etc....[19] And now, the largest abortion provider in the world has publicly declared that they are the second largest provider of chemically castrating drugs for gender-confused minors and adults in America.[20] How any of this has anything to do with "reproductive freedom for women" is anyone's guess. But it is in line with Sanger's historic commitment to sterilization and population reduction.

Beyond Planned Parenthood itself, the idea that those "less worthy" of life should be allowed to die or even actively exterminated has spread far and wide. For example, in 2016 it was reported that seventy-six percent of Neonatal Intensive Care Unit (NICU) doctors said it was ethically permissible to place a "do not resuscitate" order in the file of a child they deemed "incompatible with life"—without the parents' consent.[21] Yes, Hitlerian eugenics is still alive and well in America. But perhaps nowhere is this clearer than with the RU-486 abortion pill.

Now responsible for 63 percent of the babies murdered every year in America,[22] the sordid history of the abortion pill can be traced back to 1916. The same year that Planned Parenthood's founder opened her first "clinic" to target the "unfit," a German chemical company named I.G. Farben was established.[23] I.G. Farben would later become infamous for creating a cyanide gas known as Zkylon-B, the gas used to poison Jews in Nazi death camps.[24] The co-founder of I.G. Farben was Hoechst AG,[25] who, decades later, became the majority shareholder of a French pharmaceutical company known as Roussel Uclaf.[26] Roussel Uclaf put its initials into the murderous drug it created—RU-486. Hoechst AG simply pivoted from creating poison to murder Jews to creating poison to murder babies. It's the same company. If you think that's the product of blind chance and not that of common stakeholders engaged in the same project, I've got a bridge to sell you in Brooklyn.

One of the fruits of eugenic thought is the belief that Christian charity, rather than being a virtue, is a problem. The thinking goes like this: whenever someone helps the unemployable, the ill, the alcohol-addicted, or the feeble-minded, they are artificially rescuing those whom nature sees fit to eliminate. It's fighting against the Darwinian survival of the fittest. Not only that, but they're giving such people further opportunities to breed. So, in a society where eugenics is the guiding principle, the helpless should be left to struggle and die; prolonging their existence is neither kind nor good for the world. Can you see now why a birth control clinic in Brownsville was strategic for Sanger? The facility wasn't there to improve the plight of the "unfit"; it was there to limit their breeding.

Once again, here's Sanger in her own words:

> Even if we accept organized charity at its own valuation, and grant that it does the best it can, it is exposed to a more profound criticism. It reveals a fundamental and irremediable defect. Its very success, its very efficiency, its very necessity to the social order are the most unanswerable indictment. Organized charity is the symptom of a malignant social disease. Those vast, complex, interrelated organizations aiming to control and to diminish the spread of misery and destitution and all the menacing evils that spring out of this sinisterly fertile soil, are the surest sign that our civilization has bred, is breeding, and is perpetuating constantly increasing numbers of defectives, delinquents, and dependents. My criticism, therefore, is not directed at the failure of philanthropy, but rather at its success. These dangers inherent in the very idea of humanitarianism and altruism, dangers which have today produced their full harvest of human waste....[27]

Again, Sanger wasn't alone in her beliefs about charity. She was swimming in a stream of like-minded people, who all borrowed from men like Francis Galton and Thomas Malthus. If you recall from a previous chapter, Thomas Malthus popularized the idea that the earth could only produce so much food, so it was inevitable that a great famine would eventually wipe out millions of people and create untold suffering. Therefore, Malthus, like Sanger, explicitly argued against the work of Christian charities and ministries of mercy. He believed society should let the poor and sick die off for the greater good of humanity.

Sanger and the eugenicists of her generation were not interested in saving the poor, the ill, or the slow-witted. They were looking for commonsense ways to speed along their deaths and stop them from having children. Sanger popularized these ideas with her robust speaking schedule, her magazine, *The Birth Control Review*, and her high-profile public image. It can be argued that she did more to popularize Malthusian thought in her generation than any other single individual.

Adolf Hitler, for instance, adopted the neo-Malthusian ideas of Margaret and her friends in a wholesale fashion in his administration of the Third Reich—his exterminative "final solution"; his coercive abortion program in Poland, Yugoslavia, and Czechoslovakia; and his elitist National Socialism. He echoed the Malthusian call to "rid the earth of dysgenic peoples by whatever means available so that we may enjoy the prosperity of the Fatherland." And he reiterated the Planned Parenthood ideal of eliminating all Christian mercy ministries or social service programs. "Let us spend our efforts and our resources," he cried in a frenetic speech in 1939, "on the productive, not on the wastrel."

Josef Stalin also wove Planned Parenthood's neo-Malthusian ideal into his brutal interpretation of Marxism—his Ukrainian triage, his collectivization of the Kulaks, and his Siberian genocide. He argued that, "The greatest obstacle to the successful completion of the people's revolution is the swarming of inferior races from the south and east." And the only thing that kept him from eliminating that obstacle was "the foolhardy interference of church charity."[28]

In 1927, Margaret Sanger organized the World Population Conference in Geneva, Switzerland, the first world conference ever to deal with the "problem" of overpopulation.[29] So yes, Planned Parenthood is not merely part of the population reduction movement; they *are* the population reduction movement. The conference featured Sanger's friends from the American Eugenics Society, as well as Havelock Ellis, Julian Huxley, John Maynard Keynes, and many other eugenicists from around the globe.

Among the speakers at her conference was a certain Eugen Fischer, a professor of human genetics and racial hygiene at the University of Berlin, whose book *Principles of Human Heredity and Race Hygiene* was another prison-time favorite of Hitler's and is found referenced in *Mein Kampf*.[30] Later a member of the Nazi Party whose ideas helped craft the Nuremberg Laws of 1935, Fischer wasn't just an ideologue; he was a practitioner of the most violent forms of eugenics. Fischer had previously helped run a concentration camp in German-controlled southwest Africa before World War I, where he starved, murdered, and experimented on native Africans.[31] All of this was well documented years before the founder of Planned Parenthood asked Fischer to come and speak at her conference. One of Fischer's lectures gives us a window into the kind of individuals Sanger was eager to partner and associate with:

> I do not characterize every Jew as inferior, as Negroes are, and I do not underestimate the greatest enemy with whom we have to fight. But I reject Jewry with every means in my power, and without reserve, in order to preserve the hereditary endowment of my people.[32]

The same year he accepted Sanger's speaking invitation, Fischer became the first director of the Rockefeller-funded Kaiser Wilhelm Institute for Anthropology, Human Genetics, and Eugenics in Berlin.[33] The Rockefeller funding was used "to pay for a national survey of 'degenerative traits' in the German population."[34] Records of the Berlin Kaiser Wilhelm Institute's "activities revealed a wide range of eugenics experiments."[35] Eugen Fischer was no minor player in Hitler's Reich or "Final Solution." He was one of Hitler's most committed henchmen. At a March 1941 conference in Frankfurt addressing the "solution to the Jewish problem," Fischer "set forth ideas on eliminating Jews *en masse*. A leading idea that emerged was the gradual extinction of the Jewish people by systematically concentrating them in large labor camps to be located in Poland." However, channeling his inner Sanger, Fischer was concerned that such concentration of Jews might "lead to an increase in the birth rate." So, he insisted these labor camps consist of "unpaid slave labor" and no "improvement in living standards."[36] By 1942, "an aging Fischer" needed a replacement as Director of the Kaiser Wilhelm Institute for

Anthropology, Human Genetics, and Eugenics in Berlin. Who would replace him became a major "source of debate within eugenic and Nazi Party circles" because at this point, "Hitler's war against the Jews had escalated from oppressive disenfranchisement to systematic slaughter."[37] They needed a true believer.

Before the end of the year, Fischer had handpicked his protégé and successor. It would be Otmar von Verschuer, another eugenicist who pioneered and popularized the Nazi Party's studies on twins.[38] Von Verschuer's personal research assistant was Josef Mengele, the "Angel of Death."[39] Just six months into Von Verschuer's new position, he arranged for his faithful assistant to go to Poland. And on May 30, 1943, Mengele arrived at Auschwitz.[40] He would continue his teacher's research into twins in the most brutal, inhuman, and unspeakable ways imaginable. Mengele even sent back regular reports of his dissection of eyeballs and skulls,[41] occasionally including human samples for Von Verschuer to examine.[42] Von Verschuer was quick to thank Mengele for "the rare and valuable specimens."[43]

> In addition to eyes, Verschuer wanted blood. Liters of it. For decades, eugenicists had sought the genetic markers for "carriers," or people who appeared normal but were likely to transmit...a predisposition for a range of defective traits.... But by the twenties, the most talented eugenicists and geneticists were working hard to analyze blood serum to solve the question of defective germ plasm....They only knew that mankind's eugenic destiny was lurking in the blood and waiting to be discovered.[44]

In other words, Josef Mengele had his underlings plucking out eyeballs and draining the blood of twins at Auschwitz to send to his boss, Von Verschuer, in their eugenic pursuit of creating the master race and eliminating the "unfit."

While evidence of mass murder in the trenches of Russia and the gas chambers of Poland were systematically destroyed, Mengele's murders were enshrined in the protocols of science.

1916 AND THE RACE TO DESTROY THE "UNFIT"

Mengele's ghastly files did not remain his private mania, confined to Auschwitz. Every case was meticulously annotated, employing the best scientific method prison doctors could muster. Then the files were sent to Verschuer's offices at the Institute for Anthropology, Human Heredity, and Eugenics in Berlin for study.[45]

How does this at all differ from the abortion industry's harvesting of aborted baby parts, as they meticulously adjust how they perform abortions to deliver their victims as intact as possible, so their unspoiled organs can be sliced out and sold on the black market to researchers looking to cure diseases and create life-saving drugs? All "enshrined in the protocols of science," of course. Not by accident, the eugenicists of the abortion industry in America today share a similar fascination with the eyeballs of their victims and have been caught on camera joking about eyeballs falling into their lap as they're carefully dismembering a baby.[46] As my friend Dr. George Grant likes to say, "While Mengele and Hitler may have had a sledgehammer approach to eugenics, Sanger had more of a scalpel approach to eugenics." But make no mistake—they shared the same ideology. And Sanger was intent on ensuring Eugen Fischer was at her conference to share his "progressive" ideas!

Perfectly comfortable with Fischer's anti-black racism and murderous crimes, it should then come as no surprise that on November 21, 1930, Sanger's American Birth Control League launched a birth control clinic in Harlem, a predominantly black section of New York. The work was funded by private donors and was presented as a benefit to the citizens of the neighborhood, who did not fully comprehend the eugenics underlying the work of the ABCL. The Harlem clinic served as the test kitchen and the inspiration for the Negro Project, a full-on assault on black communities throughout the Southern United States. In proposing the Project, Sanger wrote:

> The mass of Negroes, particularly in the South, still breed carelessly and disastrously, with the result that the increase among Negroes, even more than among whites, is from that portion

of the population least intelligent and fit, and least able to rear children properly.[47]

Margaret Sanger was a racist, though it must be said Margaret Sanger wasn't a racist in the traditional sense. She did not care about the color of the black person's skin; she was concerned about their genes. Sanger believed much of the black population was simply inferior and incapable of thriving in modern society. If she had come across a black person who had bucked the trends, risen above poverty and contributed to society in a way she believed was worthy of life, Sanger would not have objected to such a person's existence. She would not have cared about the amount of melanin in their skin. Nevertheless, Sanger did believe the vast majority of African Americans were "unfit" and should not be permitted to breed.

The Negro Project carried with it a unique strategy. If you recall from the first chapter, in 1939, Sanger wrote a letter to Dr. C. J. Gamble outlining the American Birth Control League's strategy in dealing with Southern blacks:

> It seems to me from my experience where I have been in North Carolina, Georgia, Tennessee and Texas, that while the colored Negroes have great respect for white doctors they can get closer to their own members and more or less lay their cards on the table which means their ignorance, superstitions and doubts. They do not do this with the white people and if we can train the Negro doctor at the Clinic he can go among them with enthusiasm and with knowledge, which, I believe, will have far-reaching results among the colored people. His work in my opinion should be entirely with the Negro profession and the nurses, hospital, social workers, as well as the County's white doctors. His success will depend upon his personality and his training by us.[48]

One director for the Negro Project famously said, "There is a great danger that we will fail because the Negroes think it is a plan for their extermination. Hence, let's appear to let the colored run it."[49] To this day, if you walk into a Planned Parenthood in a predominantly black neighborhood, you would be welcomed by a black woman behind the desk. The strategy hasn't changed—convince vulnerable black women that the abortion clinic near their home is one vehicle where black women are helping other black women. But the truth is that Planned Parenthood locations are strategically placed in areas where people of color live.

In 2017, Life Issues Institute conducted a study on Planned Parenthood and its impact on black Americans. The study, published in 2020, revealed the following:

- 49 percent (585 of 1,189) of all zip codes within five miles of the facilities had targeted minority populations that are at least twice the national average for blacks or Hispanics/Latinos.
- Of these 585 targeted zip codes, 82 percent have minority populations greater than 50 percent, indicating robust minority communities near these facilities.
- In fact, black targeted zip codes in these counties have an average 55 percent black population and Hispanic/Latino targeted zip codes have an average 58 percent Hispanic/Latino population.
- 75 percent of abortion facilities are located within or adjacent to one of these targeted minority zip codes. These communities are a short walk or ride away from Planned Parenthood's aggressive abortion-marketing tactics and thus presumably experience a higher abortion risk.[50]

In short, Planned Parenthood places 86 percent of its abortion clinics in minority neighborhoods.[51] All these years later, the Negro Project never really ended. Sanger's legacy of targeting those she deemed "unfit" continues today.

If we look at it another way, it's even more damning. Today, just 3.5 percent of the American population are black women of childbearing age, and yet about 37 percent to 38 percent of abortions are performed on unborn black babies. What this tells us is that abortions in black communities far outpace the nation at large. Planned Parenthood, the nation's largest abortion provider, is eliminating black babies at a feverish pace. Planned Parenthood makes the KKK look mostly peaceful; they lynch more black lives in the womb every two weeks in America than the KKK lynched in a century.[52]

As I mentioned at the beginning of this book, when the Negro Project was just getting started, Sanger made use of black ministers:

> The ministers [sic] work is also important and also he should be trained, perhaps by the Federation as to our ideals and the goal that we hope to reach. We do not want word to go out that we want to exterminate the Negro population and the minister is the man who can straighten out that idea if it ever occurs to any of their more rebellious members.[53]

Sanger knew pastors and clergymen were trusted authority figures in black communities across the nation, so she used them to propagate her message. Knowing that some African Americans would naturally be skeptical of an organization whose goal was to kill their unborn, Sanger recruited black ministers who could use their pulpit and assure the masses that the abortion clinics in their neighborhoods were a blessing to alleviate poverty and extend liberty to people of color.

Today, this same kind of devilish propaganda continues. Black ministers and Christian celebrities rarely speak out in favor of abortion on demand, but they do shill for Democrat politicians who use their power, once elected, to make sure Planned Parenthood's evil work continues unabated in black communities. Christian rapper Lecrae, in the 2020 election cycle, performed at a "Get Out the Early Vote Rally and Concert" in Atlanta, Georgia, in support of then-Senate candidates and pro-abortion crazies, Raphael Warnock and Jon Ossoff. Though he later claimed he thought the event was bipartisan, it was clear by the time he arrived at the event that only Democrats were being represented.[54] Thanks to his efforts to get out the vote for candidates dedicated to enshrining Sanger's ideas in every facet of our society, both men won their Senate race against their Republican opponents. This resulted in a fifty-fifty split in the US Senate, thus ensuring Kamala Harris as the tie-breaking vote and a near-guaranteed victory for every radical, anti-God bill the Democrat Party sought to pass. I shudder to think how many black and white babies were slaughtered in the womb thanks to Lecrae's efforts to elect godless eugenicists in one of the most important Senate races in over a decade.

It's also hard to square Lecrae's statement with his previous support for Democratic gubernatorial candidate Stacey Abrams. On his Instagram account, he wrote:

> Dear @staceyabrams, My daughter looks up to you and she's 9. Not because she's familiar with your stances and policies, but because you're a highly educated woman of color who fights for what she believes in despite opposition. She sees that she can be more than what society says. Thank you.[55]

I wonder what Lecrae meant when he wrote "who fights for what she believes in despite opposition." Obviously, since he thought Ms. Abrams was a good role model for his daughter, he must appreciate something about "what she believes in." Could it be her radical pro-abortion position? How about when she said the fetal heartbeat that can be detected at six weeks is "a manufactured sound designed to convince people that men have the right to take control of a woman's body"?[56] Interestingly, after Abrams made these ridiculous comments, Planned Parenthood adjusted its website to repeat Abrams's lie:

> Planned Parenthood changed its website without any acknowledgment of modifications to say that under the five-to six-week mark of pregnancy, "a part of the embryo starts to show cardiac activity. It sounds like a heartbeat on an ultrasound, but it's not a fully-formed heart—it's the earliest stage of the heart developing." The same webpage previously said that "a very basic beating heart and circulatory system develop," per an archive of the page from July.[57]

Of course, Lecrae isn't the only Christian celebrity to embody the spirit of the Negro Project in our day. Prior to the 2022 midterm elections, Bishop T. D. Jakes of The Potter's House in Dallas, Texas, invited then-gubernatorial candidate Beto O'Rourke to appear at his church one Sunday. Though Jakes describes his political positions as conservative, he also supported Barack Obama's presidential campaigns and publicly praised Joe Biden's inaugural address.[58] It should be noted that Beto O'Rourke refused to say whether he supports *any* limits on abortion whatsoever.[59]

Jakes and Lecrae and others like them have been trusted as conservative voices in evangelical America, and yet, when the time came, they held up those who would murder our nation's children as worthy of respect—and our votes on Election Day. As my friend and brother-in-arms Pastor John Amanchukwu says, "These men are Margaret Sanger's favorite kind of negroes."[60] Just remember what Sanger wrote, "We do not want word to go out that we want to exterminate the Negro population and the minister is the man who can straighten out that idea if it ever occurs to any of their more rebellious members."

CHAPTER FIVE
1916 AND THE SEXUAL REVOLUTION

"Those who can make you believe absurdities can make you commit atrocities."

—Voltaire

In case you thought the legacy of 1916 only extended to the deaths of untold millions of babies and a racist bent that has ensured people of color have been disproportionately targeted by the demonic furor of Margaret Sanger, there's more. The seeds of the sexual revolution were also planted at 46 Amboy Street in Brownsville.

Though the sexual revolution would not blossom in the United States until the 1960s, Sanger began tilling the soil years earlier. In fact, before she set up her first birth control clinic, she was already talking about sexual liberation. You'll recall that it was Sanger's obscene sexual content that got her indicted for breaking anti-obscenity laws in New York City in 1914. In the years preceding her self-imposed exile in the United Kingdom, Sanger became fast friends with Emma Goldman, an anarchist who traveled the country speaking out against the evils of capitalism and promoting free love, birth control, and the virtues of political assassinations (when necessary). Sanger was instantly enthralled and began reading everything on Goldman's bookshelf. In fact, it was from Goldman's library that Sanger first became acquainted with the writings of the man who would one day be her lover and mentor, Havelock Ellis.

Margaret Sanger also became acquainted with Mabel Dodge, a wealthy woman who lived on Fifth Avenue and held court in her French-style salon, inviting intellectuals, activists, artists, actors, writers, and radicals to participate in an evening meal and late-night conversation. Sanger would attend and sometimes lead the discussion —and when she did, it was always about sex. Here's how Dodge described Sanger in her memoir:

> It was she who introduced us all to the idea of birth control, and it, along with other related ideas about sex, became her passion. It was as if she had been more or less arbitrarily chosen by the powers that be to voice a new gospel of not only sex-knowledge in regard to conception, but sex-knowledge about copulation and its intrinsic importance.
>
> She was the first person I ever knew who was openly an ardent propagandist for the joys of the flesh. This in those days, was radical indeed when the sense of sin was still so indubitably mixed with the sense of pleasure.... Margaret personally set out to rehabilitate sex.... She was one of its first conscious promulgators.[1]

Sanger was an advocate for all things sexual, an evangelist of the lascivious and the perverted. If it felt good—or could feel good—she was an apologist for it. Keep in mind that this was before any popular notion of free love. Sex was not talked about publicly. Any sexual activity outside of the bonds of lifelong, monogamous, heterosexual marriage was taboo. To say that Sanger was ahead of her time does not go far enough. She didn't head down a sinful trail before others did; she blazed a trail where there was none. She helped steer American culture in a direction that eventually led to the sexual revolution, with its heartbreak, surging divorce numbers, sexually transmitted diseases, abortion epidemic, and LGBTQ+ insanity. The free love movement was ultimately an attack on Judeo-Christian values, and the aftermath was no less devastating than the destruction caused by an atomic bomb.

For Sanger, unlimited sexual exploration with no taboos based on religion or generally agreed-upon morality was tied inextricably to birth control and abortion. It cannot be free love, at least not really, if there are consequences. In fact, in the very first issue of Sanger's magazine *The Woman Rebel,* the obscene content of which forced her to flee America, we find a sentence that would come to represent and encapsulate the entire Planned Parenthood philosophy to this day. She wrote, "Our objective is unlimited sexual gratification without the burden of unwanted children."[2] There you have it. The little clinic in Brownsville served as a territorial marker, a staked claim in a new culture where every desire—no matter how forbidden or sinful—could be acted upon. But the abortion business of the American Birth Control League, and later Planned Parenthood, wasn't merely a clean-up product for those who embraced the sexual revolution; Sanger and her ilk began selling sex right alongside its abortion services. The two went hand-in-hand. The more premarital sex the culture engaged in, the more abortions Planned Parenthood could sell:

> With a passionate, evangelistic zeal and a shrewd entrepreneurial effectiveness, Planned Parenthood has translated its sordid sex business into a multi-million dollar monopoly: it publishes sex-ed books, pamphlets, and curricula; it develops model sex-ed programs for communities, schools, and affiliates; it creates pre-service, in-service, and enrichment programs for sex-ed trainers; it provides a national resource clearinghouse as a conduit for the dissemination of sex-ed information and materials; it publishes journals, magazines, and newsletters to sex-ed professionals; it catalogues [sic] and evaluates all available sex-ed materials and publications; it produces films, videos, and advertisements that broadcast sex-ed themes far and wide; it advocates unrestricted sex-ed propagation—kindergarten through twelfth grade—through polit-

ical lobbying and the courts; and it sends an army of sex-ed speakers into schools, churches, and public forums every day—day in and day out.[3]

For Planned Parenthood, then and now, sex-ed is the sales funnel, abortion is their product, and our nation's children are their prospects. Lest you think I'm jesting, Planned Parenthood president Alan Guttmacher, who replaced Margaret Sanger after her death, was asked by a reporter shortly after *Roe v. Wade* was decided how he would keep the Supreme Court decision secure. He replied with just two words: "Sex education."[4] This admission from a Planned Parenthood president destroys the oft-repeated liberal argument that sex ed helps reduce the abortion rate by teaching pregnancy prevention methods. Guttmacher saw how sex ed was the linchpin of the entire abortion industrial complex. Fast-forward twenty years and former Planned Parenthood president Pamela Maraldo assured us that the strategy had not changed. "As Surgeon General Dr. Joycelyn Elders has so succinctly put it: 'We've taught our children in driver's education what to do in the front seat, and now we've got to teach them what to do in the back seat.'"[5] Though we've been conditioned to believe that most sex education is about disease prevention and the biology of sexual intercourse and pregnancy, in reality, comprehensive sex education is a religious indoctrination program. I call it one of the liturgical arms of the religion of humanism. Not coincidentally, it seemingly touches upon every aspect of our culture of death today, which was always the point. Some of its basic tenets are as follows:

- Children are naturally sexual from birth, therefore any restrictions on their sexual expression or sexual activity violate their sexual rights.
- To have good health, children and adults alike should be having regular sexual experiences either alone (masturbation) or with persons of either gender.
- A right to sexual pleasure, even at the youngest ages. is a primary human right that trumps other rights.

- Children have privacy and confidentiality rights that trump the rights of their parents to guide their education in the area of human sexuality.
- Children have a right to abortion and sexual relations without the knowledge and consent of their parents.
- Most societal sexual and gender norms, especially those based on religious beliefs. are repressive and unhealthy and should be changed.
- Children have the right to experiment with diverse sexual identities and orientations and the behaviors associated with them to develop healthy sexuality.
- Youth are to be enlisted to combat "homophobia," "transphobia," and "heterosexism" and to advocate for their sexual rights.
- Youth should be involved in the design and implementation of CSE programs.
- Children, under internationally recognized rights to health and education, have a right to all sexual information, uncensored and without parental consent.[6]

This so-called comprehensive approach to sex-ed didn't evolve naturally over time. There is, in fact, a direct line from Margaret Sanger and Planned Parenthood to this sexual propaganda. In February of 1964, the United Nations sponsored the International Symposium on Health Education, Sex Education, and Education for Home and Family Living in Hamburg, Germany. The sex-education proposal put forth by the Swedish delegates and recommended for universal use "was accepted by the majority of the delegates."[7] This is significant because in 1938, "Sweden became the first free nation in Christendom to revert to pre-Christian abortion legislation and to institutionalize Planned Parenthood's sex education and family limitation programs."[8] Sweden had already been tearing down the fruit of biblical faith and replacing it with neo-paganism for nearly three decades. The proposed program included teaching on "masturbation, abortion, birth control, and sexual deviations."[9] Just a few months after the United Nations International Symposium took place, the medical director for Planned Parenthood, Mary Calderone, left Planned Parenthood and started her own organization dedicated to radical sex education, called SIECUS, which stands for Sexuality Information and Education Council of the United States.[10] Unsurprisingly, the "SIECUS concept of sex education is a carbon copy of the Swedish program, as adopted"[11] by the United Nations.

The United Nations has long been in support of sexualizing children from a young age. Through UNESCO, the United Nations Educational, Scientific, and Cultural Organization, the UN uses the veneer of consensus and select peer-reviewed research to promote sexual liberation as a moral good for adults and children alike. As early as 1948, the director of UNESCO, Julian Huxley, worked together with G. Brock Chisholm, director of the World Health Organization (WHO) to lay the foundation for the kind of sex education that Mary Calderone would systematize at SIECUS. Upon an invitation from renowned Communist Alger Hiss, Chisholm delivered three lectures in Washington, DC, where he advocated for sex education in the schools to start as early as the fourth grade and specifically insisted on the elimination of the "ways of the elders" and the "eradication of the concept of right and wrong."[12] And guess who was serving as the chief administrator of the World Health Organization, reporting directly to G. Brock Chisholm? Frank Calderone, the husband of SIECUS founder Mary Calderone.

The United Nations and the Planned Parenthood Federation have been in bed together for a long time. So, it was only natural that Calderone would copy the UN symposium on sex-ed and bring every last bit of perversion home to the United States. In a short period, SIECUS became the leading authority on sex education in the nation and began providing materials to schools and community groups. What began at the United Nations was formalized by Planned Parenthood through SIECUS. The organization's "scientific underpinnings" came from Dr. William H. Masters and Virginia Johnson, both humanists and both researchers with the Kinsey Institute, and from the Kinsey Reports themselves. In fact, Alfred Kinsey should rightly be considered the sacred prophet behind SIECUS, UNESCO, sexual education, and the modern Left's obsessions with everything from homosexuality to pedophilia. This is why he, more than any other revolutionary figure on the Left, was given the title "father of the sexual revolution." Unsurprisingly, when Mary Calderone left Planned Parenthood to establish SIECUS, she launched it at the Kinsey Institute! The goal was clear from the beginning: teach Kinseyan sexual ethics and science as sex education for the next generation.

So, who was Kinsey? Kinsey famously conducted studies of male and female sexuality. As a zoologist and Darwinist, Kinsey originally studied the sexuality of the gall wasp. But if man is only an animal that has evolved, what's the difference between understanding the sexuality of a wasp and that of a human being? His research was—and is still— used to normalize homosexual behavior, transsexuality, and pedophilia, to mention a few perversions.

From SIECUS to Planned Parenthood to the United Nations, all of the Comprehensive Sexuality Education in our public schools today can be traced directly back to Kinsey's science and his fraudulent and vile research at the Institute for Sex Research at Indiana University. I'm not being hyperbolic. When you follow the citations, references, and studies that supposedly justify the vile and smutty sex-ed as promulgated by SIECUS and Planned Parenthood today, you'll always end up back at Kinsey. And the disciples of Kinsey know this and rejoice in it. In 2004, the Hollywood propaganda machine released the film *Kinsey* starring Liam Neeson. The film attempted to whitewash and rewrite Kinsey's life. Actress Laura Linney, who played Mrs. Kinsey in the film, later said, "Any sort of sexual education that anybody has had in the past fifty years came right from the [Kinsey] Institute.... When Kinsey published that information, he changed our culture completely."[13] No doubt intended to praise the legacy and work of Alfred Kinsey, Linney admitted what too few Christians and conservatives know—all roads lead to Kinsey.

Referring to Kinsey's research, Calderone stated that "professionals who study children have affirmed the strong sexuality of the newborn."[14] In a book written for parents, she said, "Children are sexual and think sexual thoughts and do sexual things."[15] Thus,

SIECUS has aimed to unleash the sexual nature in children, which, in their view, has been suppressed unnaturally by Christian morality. This is why, in a letter, he once wrote to his associate and sex partner Clarence A. Tripp, Kinsey conceded, "The whole army of religion is our central enemy."[16]

Within four years of the founding of SIECUS, their general information pamphlet observed "the need to understand oneself as a sexual being; that all children are born and grow up as sexual beings...."[17] The term *sexual being* is ubiquitous throughout SIECUS literature and was essentially the thesis of all of Kinsey's research. Founding board member of SIECUS Lester Kirkendall elaborates on this in the 1969 SIECUS "Study Guide No.1," saying, "Once and for all, adults must accept as fact that young people of all ages are sexual beings with sexual needs."[18] Before SIECUS had been in operation for even five years, they were publicly writing and admitting they believed children are sexual beings who have sexual needs. That is all you need to know to dismiss the entire organization and movement as a pedophilic enterprise. Fast forward to 1980 and little had changed. Speaking at an annual meeting of the Association of Planned Parenthood Physicians, Mary Calderone stated that "awareness of the vital importance of infant and childhood sexuality" was the primary goal of SIECUS.[19] Calderone even went as far as to display an ultrasound photo of a penile erection in a twenty-nine-week-old fetus at the Sixth World Congress of Sexology in Washington, DC, in May of 1983.[20] This finding was "being touted as further evidence of child sexuality."[21] This is not easy to read, but I am providing an abundance of documentation so that you might understand the depths of the evil we're dealing with in the war on our children today and how long that demonic revolution has been building.

To top it all off, the founder of SIECUS finally made a no-holds-barred defense of pedophilia:

> What do we know about situations in which young children and older people, stronger people, have had a sexual relationship of one kind or another that has been pleasant, and the child feels good about it because it's warm and seductive and

tender? If the child really enjoys this, it may be the only time the child ever gets a loving touch."[22]

If you're reading this book, you probably assume, and rightly so, that the only people who talk about children as sexual beings are pedophiles and groomers. Did I repeat myself? Vile though it may be, this is the key to understanding Planned Parenthood's radical and obscene sex-ed today. If you believe, like nearly everyone in human history before the 1940s believed, that sexuality and a sex drive do not arrive until puberty, then the only purpose in discussing sex with kids, showing pornographic cartoons to them, and explaining how to perform sexual acts is to groom them into an early exercise of sexuality. Historically, those who did that were hanged in public or beaten to a pulp, and the local law enforcement couldn't have been happier! Now, here's the key: if the pedophilic revolutionaries on the Left wanted to normalize what would have otherwise gotten them killed or chased out of town, they would need to prove that we had gotten the science of sexuality all wrong. And therefore, they would need lots of data to replace the wisdom of antiquity.

It's all due to Kinsey's books, *Sexual Behavior in the Human Male* (1948) and *Sexual Behavior in the Human Female* (1953). Kinsey interviewed more than 17,000 people throughout the course of his studies, and he reported their sexual proclivities and activities. Kinsey's defenders will tell you all the man did was report what he was told. What they fail to admit most often is that Kinsey's interviewees included prison inmates, pedophiles, and prostitutes, among other sexual deviants.

In Table 34 of his book *Sexual Behavior in the Human Male*, Kinsey charts how many orgasms children had over a twenty-four-hour period, all timed with a stopwatch. The children were between five months and ten years old. You read that right! An eleven-month-old baby had ten orgasms in an hour. Another had fourteen in thirty-eight minutes. It's all in his book. Kinsey obtained this data from sexual criminals serving life prison sentences. He argued that the children enjoyed their sexual torture and this proved children were sexual beings. His most notorious subject, interviewed in 1944, was a sexual omnivore, "'whose history of sexual encounters with men, women, boys, girls, animals and family members took 17 hours to record,' according to *The New York Times*."[23] Not only did Kinsey fail to report this subject to the proper authorities, but he also falsified data to make it appear that this one person's responses to his survey questions came from multiple people.[24] This had the effect of making the sex fiend's proclivities appear more mainstream than they, in fact, were. Kinsey never condemned this animal. Instead, he continued to solicit data from him and attempted to pay him for further research. Writing to this pedophile monster, Kinsey said, "I wish I knew how to give credit to you in the forthcoming volume for your material. It seems a shame not even to name you."[25] The data Kinsey collected was hardly based on a sample of the general population, but the results, once published, had the effect of normalizing all kinds of sexual perversion. And Kinsey was blatantly honest about his true motives. He wanted to normalize all sex acts.

In *Sexual Behavior in the Human Female*, Kinsey summed up his view of sex, comparing sexual behavior in humans to that of animals:

> Considering the physiology of sexual response and the mammalian backgrounds of human behavior, it is not so difficult to explain why a human animal does a particular thing sexually. It is more difficult to explain why each and every individual is not involved in every type of sexual activity.[26]

In other words, "You're an animal, so hump like it." Interestingly, this book was published the same year that *Playboy* was founded. Hugh Hefner dedicated his first magazine to Kinsey,[27] and he was often referred to as "Kinsey's pamphleteer." Have you ever wondered why the *Playboy* mascot is a bunny wearing a bowtie? What do bunnies do? They hump. To quote the *Playboy* mantra, "fornicate early, fornicate often, fornicate in every possible way."[28] And nearly every single photo of Alfred Kinsey shows him wearing a tweed suit and a bowtie. It was his style. *Playboy* put Kinsey's bowtie on their bunny as a tip of the hat to the man without whom they'd be nothing. Working for the Playboy Foundation, Morton Hunt wrote that the debt owed to "Alfred C. Kinsey is beyond the scope of acknowledgment; he was the giant on whose shoulders all sex researchers since his time have stood." He said they all "used his data, his thoughts, and his words every day until we supposed them our own."[29]

Now, we turn to one of the darkest and most evil events behind the entire sex-ed movement and its supposedly scientific underpinnings. As you will see, Planned Parenthood and the sexual revolution are linked once again to the Third Reich. What you must understand about Kinsey is that he lusted after sexual data, and he did not care from whom it came or how it was obtained. Enough data dressed up in the veneer of scientific inquiry could prove that everyone was born a sexual being. Once that was accomplished, everything in the culture would have to change; for that would affect our laws, education in our schools, the institution of marriage, and our understanding of human nature itself.

One of Kinsey's primary sources for his growing storehouse of sexual data was a renowned Nazi pedophile, serial rapist, and mass murderer who somehow escaped the Nuremberg Trials and was labeled by the German press as "the most important pedophile in the criminal history of Berlin."[30] His name is Dr. Fritz von Balluseck. (No, I'm not making up his last name.) Between 1942 and 1944, Dr. Von Balluseck was "the commandant of the small Polish town of Jedrzejow." In that position, he likely raped and murdered hundreds of children. Even the German news accounts reported that Von Balluseck gave children the option of him or the gas chambers.[31] However, those three years in Jedrzejow were just the tip of the iceberg for Von Balluseck's demonic hunger.

According to Dr. Judith Reisman, who devoted her entire life to exposing the fraudulent "science" and disgusting legacy of Alfred Kinsey, "Dr. von Balluseck was an incest offender who raped and sodomized not only his own offspring, but Jewish, Polish, and German children as well, from roughly 1927 to 1957."[32] Less than a year after Kinsey's death, Von Balluseck was put on trial for the sex murder of a ten-year-old girl by the name of Liselotte Hass. However, his trial quickly escalated as prosecutors uncovered the breadth of his crimes, and Von Balluseck was tried for the abuse of "more than 100" or "several hundred children." The *Frankfurter Allgemeine Zeitung* reported on May 22, 1957, that Von Balluseck had sexually violated children "over the last three decades."[33]

The trial was widely covered in Germany, and the relationship and correspondence between Kinsey and Von Balluseck soon became common knowledge. Unsurprisingly, the press in America uniformly ignored the link, and the extent of their relationship would be unknown today if it weren't for Dr. Judith Reisman's relentless research. You've probably guessed it by this point—Von Balluseck sent Kinsey pages and pages of notes detailing his sexual crimes. In their letters, Kinsey warned Von Balluseck to "watch out" lest he get caught and encouraged him to continue his research.

Reporting on Von Balluseck's trial, The *National-Zeitung* wrote on May 15, 1957, "Today the court has got four diaries, and in these diaries, with cynicism and passion, he recorded his crimes against 100 children in the smallest detail. He sent the details of his experiences regularly to the US sex researcher Kinsey. The latter was very interested and kept up a regular and lively correspondence with Balluseck."[34] The partnership between Kinsey and Von Balluseck was so self-evident that the judge in Von Balluseck's trial commented, "I had the impression that you got to the children in order to impress Kinsey and to deliver him material." Von Balluseck then replied, "Kinsey himself asked me for that."[35] So disturbed was Judge Berger after reviewing the experiments recorded in Von Balluseck's "sex diaries" that he exclaimed, "This is no longer human! What was all this for? To tell Kinsey about?"[36] Well, yes.

A Nazi pedophile, who was a serial child rapist, was one of Kinsey's researchers and pen-pals. Von Balluseck's sexual data was another scientific source used to prove Kinseyan sexual ethics—the same sexual ethics that now make up the entire foundation of Planned Parenthood and SIECUS's Comprehensive Sexuality Education throughout America's public schools.

Kinsey's sexuality was an open secret. He had many male lovers, including one Wardell Pomeroy, who was an investigator at the Kinsey Institute and later became the organization's executive director. Writing for a 1977 *Forum* publication, *Variations,* Pomeroy argued,

"Incest can be a satisfying, non-threatening and even an enriching emotional experience."[37] Pomeroy was a true believer in Kinsey's work, taking it to the logical conclusion that nothing should be off the table sexually, not even incest. Lest we conclude his was a mindset far beyond Planned Parenthood and SIECUS, it should be noted Pomeroy was an early board member of SIECUS.

Masters and Johnson, the aforementioned researchers with the Kinsey Institute, were also board members at SIECUS in the early years; and Hugh Hefner, publisher of *Playboy* magazine, provided the seed money to launch SIECUS.[38] To say that SIECUS was concerned with education rather than pushing a radical social agenda would be like saying *Playboy* was published for the articles. In recent years, even SIECUS has owned up to its role in promoting a culture of sex, branding its organization with the tagline, "Sex Ed for Social Change."[39] They're admitting in their new name what Sanger saw in 1914—the sexual revolution must always come before the social revolution. Kinsey was wrong about people being "sexual beings." However, it's self-evident that sex is a powerful aspect of human identity, for better or worse. Revolutionaries on the left have always understood that if you can titillate the masses and "incite youngsters to an emotional and sensual frenzy,"[40] they won't be able to govern themselves and will be easier to control. When the goddess of sex replaces Christendom, the revolution won't require revolutionaries anymore, because the people who now "waste away their strength in the sleep of sin and sensual pleasure" will soon "lose the power of their own initiative."[41] In *The City of God*, Augustine called it *libido dominandi*, meaning "lust of dominating," "sexual liberation as political control." Today, we might call it "the Sangerization of America."

According to Calderone:

> Curricula need to, first, *separate* kids from their parents; second, *establish* a new sexual identity for them; third, help them *determine* new value systems; and, finally, help them *confirm* vocational decisions."[42]

Planned Parenthood, the nest from which Calderone took flight to start SIECUS, will not be undone. A partner in the sexual revolution, Planned Parenthood's sex-ed curriculum is as filthy as it is undermining traditional mores—and the Bible's clear teaching—surrounding sex:

> Planned Parenthood's sex education programs and materials are brazenly perverse. They are frequently accentuated with crudely obscene four-letter words and illustrated by explicitly ribald nudity. They openly endorse aberrant behavior—homosexuality, masturbation, fornication, incest, and even bestiality—and then they describe that behavior in excruciating detail....

> "Our goal," one Planned Parenthood staffer wrote, "Is to be ready as educators and parents to help young people obtain sex satisfaction before marriage. By sanctioning sex before marriage, we will prevent fear and guilt....

> [One] Planned Parenthood publication for teens asserts: "There are only two kinds of sex: sex with victims and sex without. Sex with victims is always wrong. Sex without is always right."[43]

While the mandatory in-home learning of 2020 alerted thousands of parents in America to the vile, disgusting, and pornographic curriculum coming from Planned Parenthood and SIECUS, the truth is that such curriculum is not new; it's been in place for decades. In fact, as early as 1974, Planned Parenthood distributed a booklet to schools nationwide entitled, "You've Changed the Combination," plastered with "nude, playboy-like, huge bosomed, blond women, towering over wimpy nude males."[44] In it, Planned Parenthood encouraged children to have sex, as long as they did so only with their friends. Here's their advice:

> Do you want a warm body? Buy one. That's right. There are women who have freely chosen that business, buy one.... Do you want a virgin to marry? Buy one. There are girls in that

business too. Marriage is the price you'll pay, and you'll get the virgin. Very temporarily.

I suppose we should be thankful that Planned Parenthood's literature draws the line at rape. However, the idea that anything else goes as long as it's consensual has seeped into our culture to devastating effect. Today, our society has shifted in a way that allows all sexual activity. Leftists shout, "Love wins," and that's supposed to settle any remaining arguments. Vocalizing a biblical sexual ethic now falls into the category of hate speech. There was a time, not too long ago, when the vast majority of people in the United States believed sex should be reserved for marriage. Even when some failed to live up to this expectation, the failure wasn't flaunted. Now, traditional views are on the defensive—thanks in no small part to Sanger, Calderone, Kinsey, and others.

Of course, if you're going to promote every flavor of sex to minors —and you're a neo-Malthusian—you've got to have a solution to the "problem" of overpopulation. And that's where Sanger was uniquely positioned. Through birth control[45] and abortion, she could make sure any unwanted pregnancies were taken care of. Sanger was preaching the lie of consequence-free sex outside of marriage, and so she needed a way to deal with the consequences of her lie—abortions. So, her clinic in Brownsville was not only the first of many birth control clinics, but it was also part of the sexual revolution she helped spark.

However, many people today defend Sanger as merely a misguided, turn-of-the-century humanitarian who accidentally fell in with some very bad people in her "selfless pursuit" of helping poor women "plan" their "parenthood." In their opinion, the abortion-crazed focus of Planned Parenthood today is in no way connected to Margaret Sanger's innocent defense of birth control for the poor. While it's true that Planned Parenthood did not begin performing abortions until 1970, Sanger's hatred for babies and the abortion mindset she helped create were already full-fledged in her early writings.

In her 1931 book, *My Fight for Birth Control*, Sanger describes feeling "keen sympathy" for a drunken father, who, unable to handle the whines of his youngest baby who had eczema, had "thrown the wailing, naked infant into the snow."[46] She defends this father, saying, "Desperate for want of sleep and quiet, his nerves overcame him, and out of the door into the snow the nuisance went!"[47] In Sanger's book, infanticide is not homicide. It's just ridding yourself of a "nuisance." In fact, one year before Sanger established the organization that would later bear the name Planned Parenthood, she said something so infamous that Planned Parenthood still has to play interference to explain how it's been "taken out of context."[48] Sanger wrote, "The most merciful thing that the large family does to one of its infant members is to kill it."[49] While her defenders point to comments in which she stated she did not support abortions, her public record proves her disregard for nascent life. Addressing abortion in a debate on birth control on December 12, 1920, Sanger said:

> The only weapon that women have and the most uncivilized weapon that they have to use if they will not submit to having children every year or every year and a half, the weapon they use is abortion.... What does this mean? It means it is a very bad sign if women have to indulge in it, and it means they are absolutely determined that they cannot continue bringing children into the world that they cannot clothe, feed, and shelter. It is woman's instinct, and she knows herself when she should and should not give birth to children, and it is just as natural to trust that instinct and to let her be the one to say and much more natural than it is to leave it to some unknown God for her to judge her by. I claim it is a woman's duty and right to have for herself the right to say when she shall and shall not have children.[50]

She sounds like every mainstream Democrat today, defending abortion with comments like, "We have to trust women to make their own decisions about if and when they have children." Even many pro-lifers today deny Sanger's pro-abortion worldview. However, Sanger was quite honest. In the 1916 edition of her scandalous book *Family*

Limitation, she wrote, "No one can doubt that there are times when an abortion is justifiable."[51]

So, it should come as no surprise that shortly before founding Planned Parenthood, she wrote that abortion is simply the feminine urge for freedom:

> Being given their choice by society—to continue to be overburdened mothers or to submit to a humiliating, repulsive, painful and too often gravely dangerous operation, those women in whom the feminine urge to freedom is strongest choose the abortionist.[52]

Did you catch that? In other words, "without this basic right, women can't be free."[53] Sanger wasn't the first person to connect sexual immorality to the murder of innocent children. Those two sins have been linked together since time immemorial. In Judges 6, for example, we find the people of Israel subject to the oppression of the Midianites. This was a consequence of their sin, a judgment of God (vv. 9–10). What was their sin? They had turned aside to worship other gods. In this era, Baal and Asherah had their devotion.

Baal was a Canaanite storm god. Because the people of Israel were agrarian and dependent on the rain for their livelihood, the worship of Baal was an attempt to garner prosperity for themselves. Instead of looking to Yahweh, the true God who brings the rain, they gave themselves over to the worship of Baal. One of the things Baal required from the people, at least in certain areas and at certain times, was the sacrifice of children. He is also sometimes connected to the god Molek, another deity to whom people sacrificed their children:

> They built high places for Baal in the Valley of Ben Hinnom to sacrifice their sons and daughters to Molek, though I never commanded—nor did it enter my mind—that they should do such a detestable thing and so make Judah sin. (Jeremiah 32:35)

Baal wanted devotion. He was an imposter who sought Yahweh's throne. But he was usually not alone. His partner in crime was Asherah, a goddess who went by many names in the ancient world, including Diana and Aphrodite. Commonly called the goddess of love, she was really the goddess of sex. When she entered a culture, she brought her own sexual revolution, normally sacred prostitution, sex outside of marriage, homosexuality, transsexualism, and even incest and bestiality.

Back to Judges 6. In that famous passage, an angel of the Lord appears to a young man named Gideon and tells him that God has chosen him to face the Midianites and rescue the people of Israel. But before he faced a single Midian, the angel commanded Gideon to get a bull[54] and tear down his father's altar to Baal. Then, he was to chop down the Asherah pole next to it. After that, Gideon was to build a new altar, chop up the wood from the Asherah pole for firewood, and sacrifice the bull to Yahweh.

Symbols of the two gods stood side by side—Baal and Asherah, child sacrifice and sexual perversion. As it was in Judges 6, so it is today. The two pagan sacraments of our society are child sacrifice and sexual perversion, in worship of demon-gods. It should therefore come as no surprise that the number one provider of child sacrifice services in America today is also the number one provider of the pornographic Comprehensive Sexuality Education in America's public schools.[55] Planned Parenthood boasts of this achievement on its website.[56] Baal and Asherah again. And before God rescued His people, He demanded His servant Gideon to destroy them. God chose to deal with the Israelites' slaughter of children before anything else. It is never okay for God's people to join in the worship of false gods. It is never okay to accept child sacrifice or sexual perversion as "blessings of liberty," as David French might deem them. We need Gideons—men and women—who will destroy the altars and the symbols of worship, who will say what's unpopular in an age of idolatry. It's the only way to change the course of our history.

In 1969, a leaked Planned Parenthood memo disclosed their agenda for population control. It included, among other things:

- Educate for family limitation
- Encourage increased homosexuality
- Fertility control agents in water supply
- Encourage women to work
- Substantial marriage tax
- Eliminate welfare payments after first two children
- Compulsory abortion of out-of-wedlock pregnancies
- Compulsory sterilization for all who have two children except for a few who would be allowed three
- Confine childbearing to only a limited number of adults
- Payments to encourage sterilization
- Payments to encourage abortions
- Abortion and sterilization on demand[57]

We're still hearing this sort of rhetoric about population control. If we don't do something soon, we're told, climate change will kill us all. Human beings are the problem. We are destroying the earth. We are the enemy. Nothing has changed since this memo was issued more than fifty years ago. It's the Left's agenda. And it is entwined with Planned Parenthood's mission to reduce the number of "unfit" people. Is it any wonder that today we're still hearing calls for abortion on demand, being told about the virtues of homosexual unions, and being chastised about the selfishness of large families?

Two thousand years ago, Jesus said, "By their fruit you will recognize them" (Matthew 7:16a). Well, we've had more than a hundred years to get to know the fruit of Margaret Sanger—and it's rotten to the core. Today's progressive culture is her dream come to life, and it's a restless poison that will not stop permeating every aspect of life— that is unless people who love truth and goodness stand up. We must push back the evil that emanated from Sanger's original birth control clinic. In short, we must undo 1916.

CHAPTER SIX
WOKE AS WOLVES

"We simply found ourselves in contact with a certain current of ideas and plunged into it because it seemed modern and successful.... You know, we just started automatically writing the kind of essays that got good marks and saying the kind of things that won applause.... We were afraid of a breach with the spirit of the age, afraid of ridicule.... Having allowed ourselves to drift, unresisting...accepting every half-conscious solicitation from our desires, we reached a point where we no longer believed the Faith."

—C. S. Lewis

The eighteenth-century philosopher Jean-Jacques Rousseau, whose ideas fomented the French Revolution, was no fan of the Christian faith. Writing about the Christians he observed in his day, he wrote:

> The country of the Christian is not of this world. He does his duty, indeed, but does it with profound indifference to the good or ill success of his cares. Provided he has nothing to

reproach himself with, it matters little to him whether things go well or ill here on earth. If the State is prosperous, he hardly dares to share in the public happiness, for fear he may grow proud of his country's glory; if the State is languishing, he blesses the hand of God that is hard upon His people.... If the power is abused by him who wields it, it is the scourge wherewith God punishes His children. There would be scruples about driving out the usurper: public tranquility would have to be disturbed, violence would have to be employed, and blood spilt; all this accords ill with Christian meekness; and after all, in this vale of sorrows, what does it matter whether we are free men or serfs? The essential thing is to get to heaven, and resignation is only an additional means of doing so.... Christianity preaches only servitude and dependence. Its spirit is so favourable to tyranny that it always profits by such a régime. True Christians are made to be slaves, and they know it and do not much mind: this short life counts for too little in their eyes.[1]

Though these words are more than 250 years old, they could have been written about Christianity in the West today. Just look at so-called Christian leaders, and by and large, you'll find one commonality—no one wants to fight.

Up until now, we've been looking at the vile plans of the Left that have been realized over the past century or so. These Marxist revolutionaries have not hesitated to fight for their values and beliefs. But Christians? As a group, we have largely played to get along, remained silent as our culture descended into drag-queen-story-hour nonsense and transgender savagery, and comforted each other with platitudes like, "After all, Jesus *said* the world would hate us," as though that means we should be cheering as our once God-fearing nation becomes ever more hostile to Christianity and the clear teachings of Scripture.

It's often in the name of the Great Commission that pastors, teachers, and Christian celebrities step back from the culture war. For the sake of evangelism and the reputation of the church, these men and women fail to speak out against the culture of death. They dare not say a word about the division and utter destruction caused by the grift that is Black Lives Matter, Inc. lest they get tagged as racist. They don't advocate for laws that will stem the holocaust of abortion, so as not to upset those who champion the murder and mutilation of the unborn. And they don't declare God's design for gender, marriage, and identity, but instead, consider using someone's preferred pronouns as a way of loving their neighbor.

All of these nods and winks at evil will open the door for the gospel in American life, they tell us. Our silence and acquiescence will win people over so that we have opportunities to share the good news with people in desperate need. Only, that never happens. It turns out that staying cool while young boys and girls are pumped full of hormones and have their genitals chopped off isn't the open door to evangelism they imagine it is. The Great Commission will never be completed by placating men and women who despise Christian values. In addition, if you pay attention to what Jesus commanded His followers to do, you'll realize that even if it were possible, we have not been given the option of sacrificing the nation to save a few select souls. Here's what Jesus actually said:

> "All authority in heaven and earth has been given to me. Therefore go and make disciples of all nations, baptizing them in the name of the Father and of the Son and of the Holy Spirit, and teaching them to obey everything I have commanded you. And surely I am with you always, to the very end of the age." (Matthew 28:18b–20)

Jesus has complete and total authority. That is why He is not content with a few scattered disciples throughout the world. He told His followers to go out and make disciples of entire nations, transforming society, upending politics as usual, and bringing every sphere of culture under His active reign. And it's not just about folks self-identifying as Christian in surveys; Jesus wants them to "obey everything" He commanded. This is why, at the end of history, we will be able to say, "The kingdom of the world has become the kingdom of our Lord and of his Messiah" (Revelation 11:15b).

Are you catching the radical nature of this grand assignment? Christians have not been given the option to sit on the sidelines while the world burns. We have no choice but to be witnesses for Christ everywhere and by every means. We are to testify to the truth with our words and with our actions, whether the world appreciates that truth or not. And we are to push back against the darkness, even if the people around us curse the light. Of course, we must be wise in how we fulfill our calling, but that doesn't mean we can neglect the Lord's directive to make disciples of all nations.

It's hard to argue with someone who says they're leading their ministry a certain way for the sake of evangelism. For many people, the conversation ends right there. What could be more important than rescuing souls from the eternal fires of hell? But the compromise we see today is rarely about soul winning; more often it's about money and status and getting invited to all the cool parties.

Now, of course, no one can peer into another's soul to see their true motivations. However, we can look at observable patterns of behavior and who is rewarded for certain activities. For example, there's a reason that when MSNBC wants a "conservative" Christian response on an issue of the day, they'll tag Russell Moore and not Jack Hibbs. There's also a reason David French has an opinion column in *The New York Times* and Eric Metaxas doesn't.

Just as Margaret Sanger once used black ministers as trusted community leaders to push her abortion agenda, now the Left uses token conservatives to push their vile policies. The trick is that the conservative must only punch to the right. They can criticize other Christian leaders, the people in the pews, and the oddities of the Christian subculture, but they can never offer clear biblical responses to the issues. Heck, they don't even have to echo the Leftist propaganda; they just have to provide cover for it. In other words, French doesn't have to say drag-queen-story-hour is morally neutral or that it aligns with his Christian beliefs; he just has to say it's "one of the blessings of liberty."[2] French was certainly ridiculed by actual conservatives —and even liberals with common sense—for this sound bite, but the mainstream media and cultural elites lauded him for it. And that's how the game is played: French gets to keep calling himself a Christian conservative, all the while aiding and abetting those who would spit in the face of Christ, and he receives a handsome earthly reward for his service.

———

More than 2,500 years ago, the people of Judah were taken into exile in Babylon. Shortly thereafter, the prophet Jeremiah wrote a letter to his kinsmen who had been marched off to a foreign land. In the letter, he conveyed God's promise that when seventy years had passed, He would bring His people back to the land of promise (Jeremiah 29:10). But seventy years is a long time to wait, so the Lord told them that in the meantime they should "seek the peace and prosperity of the city to which I have carried you into exile. Pray to the LORD for it because if it prospers, you too will prosper" (Jeremiah 29:7).

As Christians in this world, there's a sense in which we're living in exile. This world, as it currently exists, is not our home. But that doesn't mean we can afford to run out the clock, waiting for God's rescue. We, too, are called to "seek the peace and prosperity" of the cities where we find ourselves. And not just the cities, but the nation, and by extension, the whole world.

We are to contend for godly ideas and policies that align with biblical values upstream so that human lives are not wrecked downstream. That is how we seek peace and prosperity. That is how we provide for human flourishing. But all too often the church has been content to set up shop downstream, bandaging those who have been devastated by wicked policies. It's a wonderful thing to counsel women who are brokenhearted because they had an abortion. But do you know what's better? Helping create a culture through policy and persuasion where such counseling isn't needed anymore. It's an important ministry to help detransitioners heal from the trauma of their chemical and surgical castration and mutilation and come to terms with the fact that they can never have children. But do you know what's better? Getting godly men elected who will ban such horrors from happening in the first place. It's a godly and honorable thing to operate a soup kitchen for the homeless. But do you know what's better? Advocating for tax policies that encourage full employment; fighting for an end to pointless foreign wars after which many of our bravest citizens come home with mental health problems; and voting for candidates who will secure our borders to squeeze out the flow of drugs from South America and China.

We talk about a *culture war*, but that term is misleading. It would imply that there is a battle being waged between two factions within our society. But the truth is, the church hardly fights at all. The most well-known and prominent Christians in our nation, instead of rallying people to the cause of justice, are too busy telling rank-and-file believers they can, in good conscience, vote for the party that wants to lynch babies in the womb. They are silent on the issues that matter most to God, and they are more than happy to baptize progressive talking points when it suits their platform and position.

One terrifying example is the late Tim Keller, the founding pastor of Redeemer Presbyterian Church in New York City, co-founder of The Gospel Coalition, and the author of several bestselling books, including *The Reason for God*. Keller earned a reputation as a thinking man's preacher and a solid Bible teacher. In fact, for many years, he was held up as an example of what a Christian minister in our postmodern world ought to be like. *Newsweek* even dubbed Keller "the C. S. Lewis for the twenty-first century." You may be reading this and feel tempted to close the book right now, as Pastor Tim Keller is a hero to many conservative, pro-life, evangelical Christians, and I have taken plenty of heat for saying on stage what you're about to read. But I ask you to continue reading because this is too important to remain willfully ignorant about.

In a 1999 piece for *Christianity Today* entitled, "Religion-Less Spirituality," Keller wrote the following:

We will be careful with the order in which we communicate the parts of the faith. Pushing moral behaviors before we lift up Christ is religion. The church today is calling people to God with a tone of voice that seems to confirm their worst fears. Religion has always been outside-in—"If I behave out here in all these ways, then I will have God's blessing and love inside." But the gospel is inside-out—"If I know the blessing and grace of God inside, then I can behave out here in all these ways."

A woman who had been attending our church for several months came to see me. "Do you think abortion is wrong?" she asked...

I said that I did.

"I'm coming now to see that maybe there is something wrong with it," she replied, "now that I have become a Christian here and have started studying the faith in the classes."

As we spoke, I discovered that she was an Ivy League graduate, a lawyer, a long-time Manhattan resident, and an active member of the ACLU. She volunteered that she had experienced three abortions.[3]

Let's hold it right there for a moment. First of all, notice that Keller divorced proclaiming Christ from moral behavior. This is, in and of itself, foreign to the teaching of the Bible. In Scripture—in both the Old and New Testaments—godly behavior, and careful obedience to God's moral standards, was one of the ways believers honored God. But Keller is saying we should not address moral behaviors at all. Do you remember when Jesus did not condemn the woman caught in adultery in John 8? It wasn't that He thought she should wait to address her immoral behavior until sometime later when she felt secure in God's love. No, He told her, "Go now and leave your life of sin" (John 8:11b).

Second, notice how Keller speaks about the woman's abortions. She "experienced" three abortions. He's using a euphemism to take the power out of the woman's actions. It was her unborn children who "experienced" the abortions. They experienced having their young lives snuffed out, their bodies burned and dismembered. Imagine saying that a plantation owner in the antebellum South "experienced" slavery. No, he wasn't owned by another human being. He wasn't whipped, chained, or forced to labor for no pay. He didn't "experience" slavery; he enslaved his fellow divine image-bearers—and profited from it. He is guilty of great sin, just as is the woman who aborted three of her children in Keller's story. Keller's choice of words here reveals his dismissive attitude toward the plight of the unborn.

Back to the article:

"I want you to know," she said, "that if I had seen any literature or reference to the 'pro-life' movement, I would not have stayed through the first service. But I did stay, and I found faith in Christ. If abortion is wrong, you should certainly speak out against it, but I'm glad about the order in which you do it."[4]

Keller's point is clear: we should avoid speaking about moral behaviors from the pulpit because it will drive people away from the gospel—people like the woman in his story. So, there can't be teaching on abortion, sexual sin, transgenderism, or anything of the sort, because the gospel witness will be harmed. Had Keller lived in the days leading up to the Civil War, would he have preached against the evils of slavery? Of course not. Rather, he'd share a "clean" gospel, free of morality, in the hope that sometime later, the slaveholders in his congregation would come to realize, on their own, the wickedness of owning other human beings. In our day, clerical silence in the face of child sacrifice is perfectly acceptable, even preferable. The last thing we want to do is use the influence of our pulpits, our platforms, and our positions to help put an end to abortion in America.

Keller, who was a registered Democrat, at least in his later years,[5] took to Twitter to say that Christians have "freedom of conscience" when it comes to voting. "The Bible tells me that abortion is a sin and great evil, but it doesn't tell me the best way to decrease or end abortion in this country, nor which policies are most effective...this means when it comes to taking political positions, voting, determining alliances and political involvement, the Christian has liberty of conscience."[6] In other words, "If you feel okay about voting for pro-abortion Democrats who lynch babies in the womb, then that's okay. That's between you and God."

Once again, let's apply Keller's logic to a previous era. According to him, it would have been acceptable for followers of Christ to support the Democrat party of the 1850s. After all, the Bible doesn't give us policy prescriptions to decrease slavery. So, it would have been perfectly fine to vote for Stephen Douglas, who ran against Lincoln. He was a racist who wanted to keep slavery in perpetuity, but it would have been perfectly fine to back his ticket because Christians have "freedom of conscience" to vote however they wish. What about German Christians in the 1930s? Would it have been acceptable for them to support Adolf Hitler? According to Keller, sure! The Bible doesn't say what policies will end the Holocaust soonest, so no one needs to feel pressured to take any one political side on the issue. Liberty of conscience!

Of course, Keller would have said—and did say[7]—that slavery and the Holocaust were both evil. However, he places them in a different category than abortion because he believes it's permissible for Christians to support political candidates who champion the practice and want to keep it legal. But all three—the owning of slaves, the systematic eradication of Jews, and the slaughtering of the unborn—have one thread in common. Each one begins by denying personhood to the victims.

In 2018, Keller wrote, "Those who avoid all political discussion and engagement are essentially casting a vote for the status quo.... To not be political is to be political."[8] And yet, as we have already discussed, he was more than happy to instruct Christians to remain silent on the issue of abortion and to freely vote for the Democrat party. Why? Because being against abortion is not a politically correct position to take in our culture today, and being a Democrat puts a person in sync with the power centers of our day—the mainstream media, Hollywood, and Keller's own New York City. So, no, Tim Keller was not a godly, moral voice for our age; he was a wolf in sheep's clothing who led many Christians into error and who provided cover for some of the greatest villains of our time. When it counted the most, he revealed himself to be both a hypocrite and a coward.

As I mentioned briefly in chapter three, the majority of pastors in Nazi Germany were not willing to speak up against the atrocities of Hitler's regime. They were cowardly and missed the moment for which God had called them, but more than that, they chose cultural acceptance over the kingdom of God. Many perks and privileges came with tacitly supporting the Nazi agenda, even if that support only came through silence. These Lutheran ministers enjoyed relative comfort and peace and, until the war came home, fashionable parties and the company of the elites.

Likewise, there are benefits given to American pastors and evangelical leaders who support the Marxist vision for a new society. They enjoy perks and privileges while rubbing elbows with political and cultural elites. Their names adorn bylines in the most fashionable magazines and newspapers. They're invited to be guests on Sunday morning news programs and primetime opinion shows. They might even find themselves in a Rob Reiner documentary mocking all those backward Christians who believe in "Christian nationalism," loosely defined as any effort to restrict abortion access or end the mutilation of children in the name of so-called transgender rights.[9]

The lure of these cultural perks is strong—so strong that once decent, God-fearing men and women are willing to look the other way when it comes to the most gruesome of abominations. We know this because, following the onset of the COVID-19 pandemic, several Christian leaders—all of the same ilk—lent their platforms to Francis Collins, then the director of the National Institutes of Health (NIH). They vouched for Collins, celebrated his work, heralded him as a brother in Christ, and used their authority and credibility to push his health directives onto their unsuspecting followers.

"Collins isn't just any government scientist," they said. "He's one of us," they told their audiences. "He's a Christian. You can trust him." True enough. Francis Collins does claim to be a Bible-believing Christian, but as we'll see, his actions as director of the NIH reveal a person who is anything but a follower of Christ.

Let's start with something so disgusting and immoral that it defies explanation. In fact, if it weren't so well documented it might have fallen into the mirky abyss of urban legend. But it's absolutely true.

> In the fall of 2020, researchers at the University of Pittsburgh published a study titled, "Development of humanized mouse and rat models with full-thickness human skin and autologous immune cells." In studying how organs reacted to pathogens or infections on human skin, researchers grafted "full-thickness human skin" as well as thymuses, livers, and spleens from fetuses onto rodent bodies, creating what they call "humanized rat models."[10]

Humanized rats. That's what these mad scientists were after. They purchased the murdered remains of God's image-bearers from a local Planned Parenthood butcher shop, then sliced off the scalps and attached them to the heads of lab rats. This is the kind of thing that would make Joseph Mengele blush. It's hard to imagine anything more macabre. As head of the NIH, not only did Collins approve this study, thus validating its objectives, but he also provided taxpayer funds to pay for it. How does a Christian—a man who calls himself a disciple and servant of Jesus Christ—reconcile this wickedness with the Bible's teaching on the sanctity of human life? One year later, thanks to the brave work of pro-life undercover journalists, the University of Pittsburgh admitted to removing the kidneys from born-alive babies while their hearts were still beating. David Daleiden, who helped expose the University of Pittsburgh discovered that "Pitt and the Planned Parenthood abortion providers responsible for its 'research' abortions are allowing babies, some at the age of viability, to be delivered alive, and then killing them by cutting their kidneys out" for NIH grant money.[11] Collins used his post at the NIH to provide nearly $3 million to the University of Pittsburgh for this program. The university used those funds to develop a "tissue hub" harvested from the organs of fetuses ranging from six weeks to forty-two weeks in gestation.[12] In other words, some of the babies they were picking apart were full-term and viable by any medical standard. They could have—and should have—been provided with a safe birth and placed in a loving home, but instead were murdered and scavenged for parts. Yet, Collins calls himself pro-life, as though the term has almost no meaning whatsoever. And there's more to Collins's pro-life record:

> Collins championed the unrestricted funding of embryonic stem-cell research, which involves the destruction of human embryos.
>
> Collins has even declined to condemn eugenic abortions of infants with Down's Syndrome, telling Beliefnet.com that "in our current society, people are in a circumstance of being able to take advantage of those technologies [i.e., abortions]. And we have decided as a society that that choice needs to be defended."[13]

During the COVID-19 pandemic, Collins demanded that churches stay shuttered until at least the fall of 2021.[14] He also advocated for strict vaccine mandates, even telling MSNBC:

> For me, this is really an occasion to think about loving your neighbor, not just yourself.... If we really want to get through this, we've got to figure out how those 80 million people who still haven't rolled up their sleeves, can see this as an opportunity and a responsibility not just about them....
>
> And this culture war, in this case, is killing people. It's not just a philosophical political argument. It's killing people, including, I'm sad to say, some children. We have to get past this if we

really have a future as a nation. And history is going to look back on this. And maybe I would like to say particularly to those leaders who are on the wrong side of this, what Lincoln said one time. Citizens, we will not escape history. Do you want to be looked at in the lens of that backward look ten years from now and defend what you did when in fact, we are losing tens of thousands of lives that didn't have to die.[15]

That's right. Collins said that the decision not to accept an experimental "vaccine" to treat a disease with a 97 percent survival rate—a "vaccine" that, as it turned out, did not prevent transmission or infection—was a failure to love your neighbor. He went on cable television and told the nation that not only would it be a sin to refuse the "vaccine" but also that it would kill children. What he didn't tell you, and what most Americans still don't know to this day, is that without the killing of children, there would be no COVID pandemic and no "vaccine." Both the SARS-CoV-2 virus and the "vaccine" could not have been created without aborted children.

Here's what happened: we know now that COVID-19 was due to gain-of-function research. That's the intentional creation of superviruses for the supposed purpose of finding cures before such viruses arise naturally. It's getting clearer and clearer that it was this type of research at the Wuhan Institute of Virology in China that led to a lab leak, which created the COVID pandemic.

After smearing anyone who thought COVID-19 came from a lab as a dangerous, anti-science, conspiracy theorist, President Biden's administration admitted that COVID-19 was "probably"[16] due to a lab leak and not a bat bite. Kansas Senator Roger Marshall released a three-hundred-page report on the origins of COVID-19 in 2023 and said the evidence of a lab leak is so overwhelming that 95 percent of the evidence supports the lab leak theory.[17] So what were they doing at the Fauci/Collins-funded Wuhan Institute of Virology that led to the escaped virus? They were performing experiments with humanized mice, the same kind created at the University of Pittsburgh and funded by Collins's NIH.

Humanized mice are created by nuking their immune systems and introducing peripheral blood mononuclear cells (PBMCs) to create a humanized model. The experts of this particularly grisly process did their work at the University of North Carolina at Chapel Hill. Dr. Lishan Su from UNC at Chapel Hill admits that nothing works for creating humanized mice quite as well as using the bodies and cells from aborted children. He says, "Using fetal tissue is not an easy choice, but so far there is no better choice...many, many biomedical researchers depend on fetal tissue research to really save human lives...and I think many of them feel the same way."[18]

What you likely haven't heard in the legacy media is that it was Dr. Lishan Su's supervisors, Dr. Vineet Menachery and Dr. Ralph Baric at UNC at Chapel Hill, who first engineered the bat virus in 2015, making it transmissible to humans via experiments with mice that had been humanized through fetal tissue-derived fetal clone serum and the HEK-293 cell line. HEK-293 is the infamous cell line cloned from a murdered baby named Johanna Vera Alderliesten. In 1972, Professor Alex van der Eb worked with an abortionist to deliver Johanna, likely alive, and harvest her kidney.[19] Johanna's cloned kidney was used to develop or test three of the four COVID "vaccines," while the fourth used stem cells from a different aborted baby.[20] Johanna's cloned kidney also was used to "humanize" the rats, enabling the cross-species transmission of COVID-19 from bat to human.[21]

Despite the US government's imposed moratorium on federal funding of such gain-of-function research in 2014, the NIH allowed the Menachery/Baric study to proceed under review.[22] Bet you can't guess who was leading the NIH at the time and allowed the study that first made a wild bat coronavirus transmissible to humans? Francis Collins. In fact, as early as May of 2020, we knew the Wuhan Institute of Virology was using humanized mice procured from UNC at Chapel Hill.[23] Dr. Kathleen Ruddy, a former member of the Leadership Council of the Harvard School of Public Health, was one of the first doctors to observe the undeniable link between abortion and the creation of SARS-CoV-2. "We've got fetal tissue rocking through the creation of the agent that was let loose on the world and has devastated the world," she grimly concluded. Dr. Ruddy explains that "the wild bat coronavirus could not have made its cross-species transmission without the use of fetal tissue. Mice humanized with fetal tissue-derived agents are the intermediate vector which made the COVID-19 pandemic possible."[24] No abortion, no COVID-19 pandemic.

I'm afraid it gets worse. As Dr. Ruddy further explains, "Because SARS-CoV-2 was generated in humanized mice, it tends to 'stick' to them and flourishes in them. That makes all the COVID-19 medical interventions dependent on humanized mice. So, the initial entailment with murder forces us to continue cooperating with this evil, to find treatments most easily."[25] In other words, because SARS-CoV-2 originated in humanized mice, testing for vaccines and treatments must also be on humanized mice if we're to create the most effective drug. However, these Nazi-esque scientists weren't satisfied with humanized mice only created with little Johanna's cloned kidney. They wanted new and fresh aborted children to create their Frankenstein rats, using experiments nearly identical to those employed by Collins's friends and grant recipients at the University of Pittsburgh. Besides their baby-Johanna-derived humanized mice, which are responsible for COVID-19, Dr. Robert Baric and his team at UNC at Chapel Hill also have created humanized mice with the actual organs of recently aborted babies. Their lung-only mouse (LoM) was created by implanting human fetal lung tissue on the backs of lab rats, and their BLT-L mouse (bone marrow, liver, thymus, lung) was created by engrafting such murdered baby organs under the renal capsule of the mouse.[26] Published in *Nature Biotechnology* magazine on August 26, 2019,[27] the purpose of this study was "to test vaccines for the treatment of coronavirus"[28] and was funded by an NIH grant.[29] Francis Collins again. Planned Parenthood profits from all of this of course, as they help provide a fresh supply of murdered babies. Dr. Baric's lung-only mouse model was made "using fetal tissue from the infamous Advanced Bioscience Resources (ABR), whom Judicial Watch and The Center For Medical Progress have exposed for illegal organ trafficking in partnership with Planned Parenthood."[30] Dr. Baric's LoM model was also used in another UNC at Chapel Hill study in February of 2021, this time to test the COVID-19 antiviral pill Molnupiravir.[31] The study reported that "lung tissue from at least 12 aborted babies was used" and these babies were between sixteen and twenty-two weeks of gestation. Francis Collins's research demands a fresh supply of murdered babies, and he has been funding such deadly experiments since before the COVID-19 pandemic. In 2019, "the NIH awarded $109 million in taxpayer funds for grants to 135 researchers at 65 different academic organizations for experiments using fetal organs—eyes, brains, urinary tract tissue, intestines, hearts, gonads, livers, and thymuses from aborted babies."[32] And guess who the top recipient of those millions was? The University of North Carolina at Chapel Hill, which received a staggering $10 million.

The body of research required to create the COVID-19 "vaccines" required the continued murder of preborn children, whose organs were needed to create enough humanized mice to complete the testing of the four "vaccines." No abortion, no vaccine. When Francis Collins told the world that refusing to take a COVID-19 "vaccine" would kill children, the truth was he was helping kill children to create those "vaccines," all while trying to cover up his role in the SARS-CoV-2 outbreak.

At the same time, he was fine with denying Christians their First Amendment rights. On top of all of this, Collins used his post to suppress the lab-leak theory of the virus's origin, impeding true scientific inquiry and manipulating public opinion toward the government's official narrative—a narrative that failed to mention US taxpayer funding of the Wuhan Institute of Virology.[33]

In addition, here are some other "achievements" from Collins's time heading the NIH, and they're hardly what you would expect from someone who claims to bend his knee to Jesus as Lord of all:

- Record-level spending on scientific experimentation performed on fetuses obtained from abortions
- Endorsement of unrestricted funding of embryonic stem cell research
- Millions of dollars in taxpayer grants spent on transgender research on minors
- Opposite-sex hormone treatments given to children as young as eight years old

- Mastectomies performed on girls as young as thirteen years old
- Millions of dollars in grants to an app program that tracked teenage boys' homosexual activities including anal sex, all without parental knowledge[34]

In case you thought Collins only deviated from the teaching of Scripture when it came to issues that butted up against science, he also parrots other Leftist lies, including the oft-repeated fabrication that our country is structurally and irreparably racist. Collins speaks of "equity" rather than "equality" whenever the subject is broached. He even required scientists seeking grants from the NIH to pass diversity, equity, and inclusion training first.[35] On top of that, Collins considers himself an "ally" of the LGBTQ+ community, writing:

> I applaud the courage and resilience it takes for individuals to live openly and authentically, particularly considering the systemic challenges, discrimination, and even violence that those and other underrepresented groups face all too often. As a White cisgender and heterosexual man, I have not had the same experiences, but I am committed to listening, respecting, and supporting those individuals as an ally and advocate. I know that developing allyship is critical as we continue to make NIH, and the world, a more inclusive place for all.[36]

Despite this abysmal track record, Francis Collins is a darling of Big Eva (Big Evangelicalism) elites. Lauded as a hero of the faith because he professed belief in God while leading the Human Genome Project some years back, Collins became a link between Christian institutions and the scientific establishment. Being associated with Collins meant a pastor couldn't be some backward-thinking fundamentalist, so Collins's image became synonymous with a more nuanced, reasonable faith—perhaps even a faith that was academically robust.

A hundred years ago, the Fundamentalist-Modernist controversy divided the church in America, leaving the fundamentalists with their literal interpretation of the Bible and the modernists wallowing in progressivism and suckling at the teat of scientific inquiry, which at the time included a generous helping of eugenics.[37] In time, the modernists abandoned anything that could be mistaken for orthodox Christian faith. Neo-evangelicalism, which emerged a few decades later, was an attempt to make Christianity culturally relevant once again. Harold John Ockenga, Carl F. H. Henry, and Billy Graham were architects of the movement in the early days. The plan was simple: hold on to the theological convictions of the fundamentalists while engaging culture in such a way that non-Christians would look in from the outside and want to follow Jesus.[38]

Though the stated goal was to win souls for Christ while transforming the culture for Jesus, it's easy to see how the ambition of many became mere cultural relevance and acceptability. They wanted a seat at the table. All these years later, the battle for souls and the culture has been all but abandoned by evangelical elites; the only prize they seem interested in is cultural acceptability. So, as our culture grows more and more pagan, the lengths these wolves will go to have only grown. This is why they welcome a man like Francis Collins with open arms. He represents approval by the establishment. After all, he's kind of a big deal; he was on the cover of *Time* magazine.[39] Here are just a few of the things said about the man:

- In October of 2021, after news of the humanized rat experiments became public, Russell Moore, then public theologian for *Christianity Today* (now the editor-in-chief of the publication), said of Collins, "I admire greatly the wisdom, expertise, and, most of all, the Christian humility and grace of Francis Collins. I cannot wait to see how God uses him next."[40] It's worth noting that this is not the first time that supposedly "pro-life advocate" Russell Moore has platformed those who support the legal right to murder babies. In 2017, while president of the Ethics & Religious Liberty Commission of the Southern Baptist Convention, Dr. Moore hosted an Evangelicals for Life conference. Advertised as a pro-life conference during the March for Life week outside of Washington, DC, Russell

Moore featured Pastor Eugene Cho, the former lead pastor of Quest Church in Seattle. I was in attendance at the conference and heard Pastor Cho's talk. He criticized pro-lifers for not doing enough to protect other lives and insisted that "all life is sacred and every single human being bears the image of God."[41] However, what Dr. Moore didn't tell attendees is that Cho believes it should be legal to murder pre-born children. Long before the conference, Cho wrote on his website, "I am against abortion. However, I just do not believe we can legislate it.... Can we maintain choice but do all that we can to preserve and ensure the life of an unborn?"[42] In other words, pre-born babies don't have enough value to warrant legal protection. Like his indefensible support of Francis Collins, Dr. Moore has never apologized for platforming Eugene Cho.

- Rick Warren, former pastor of Saddleback Church in Orange County, California, and author of the bestselling book *The Purpose-Driven Life*, identifies himself as a friend of Collins. In a podcast hosted by the Department of Health and Human Services, he said, "We have been friends—he and I've been friends—for many, many years. I think we first met years ago when we were both speaking at the Davos World Economic Forum. And we were two of the few Christians that were actually there at the time. And we just hit it off and spent some time together while we were there. I want to say I personally know Francis Collins to be a man of integrity. He is a man that you can trust.... He's a Christian brother in Christ."[43]

- *The New York Times* columnist and perpetual punch-to-the-right hired gun David French called Collins "a national treasure" and thanked him for his service.[44] Again, this was *after* reports about the baby scalping and tissue harvesting went public. But don't worry, David

French says he's a born-again evangelical Christian.

- In 2021, Michael Gerson, former speechwriter for the George W. Bush White House and columnist for *The Washington Post* (now deceased), wrote, "In Collins, restless genius is other-centered…a life so relentlessly committed to the human good."[45] Just not for the good of unborn humans.

Everyone remembers the haze of false information swirling around in the early months of the COVID-19 pandemic. It was difficult to separate fact from fiction or to know who could be trusted. So, it would be forgivable if a few Christian leaders or well-known pastors said something that turned out to be misinformation. But it wasn't just a few, and it wasn't just for the first few months of the crisis. In addition to the men listed above, notables like Tim Keller, Ed Stetzer, and N.T. Wright also platformed and gushed over Francis Collins. To date, **none of these men has apologized for his full-throated endorsement of Collins or the abuse of his spiritual authority.** Remember—these men didn't just offer space for Collins to offer his opinion; they made false equivalencies.

For example, Stetzer, then the executive director of the Billy Graham Center at Wheaton College and currently the dean of the Talbot School of Theology at Biola University, parroted Collins's line about getting the COVID jab being the equivalent of loving your neighbor. He also publicly chastised conservative Christians for being "conspiracy theorists," saying, "If you want to believe that some secret lab created this as a biological weapon, and now everyone is covering that up, I can't stop you."[46] Interestingly enough, the *Christianity Today* article in which Stetzer told Christians to "repent" for sharing the lab-leak theory has now been taken down.[47] No correction. No update. No apology. You have to go to the Wayback Machine to find it. It's a scandal when *The New York Times* has more journalistic integrity than the Christian publication co-launched by Billy Graham.

Now, of course, we know that the NIH funded gain-of-function research at the Wuhan Lab, so Collins was conducting his media tour, which targeted the support of Christian leaders under false pretenses. He had something to cover up. And we also know the lab leak theory was suppressed by the US intelligence community.[48] But no Christian leader has come forward to ask for forgiveness for their part in the propaganda campaign. No one has mentioned that perhaps Francis Collins doesn't show the genuine fruit of following Christ. None of these supposedly godly Christian leaders has anything to say about his "brother in Christ" funding the live dissections of infants for fresh organs, sexualizing teenage boys, carving the breasts off of healthy teenage girls, chemically castrating children, praising eugenic abortions, and buying the organs of our preborn brothers and sisters, whose continued bloodshed was required for the creation of the "vaccines." It's all crickets.

Why? Because it was never about being winsome, speaking the truth in love, or promoting goodness in the world. It was never about following Jesus or shepherding the flock. It was about gaining respectability in the right circles. Since that was achieved, there's nothing more to say on the subject. Let me repeat those names. Pastor Tim Keller, Pastor Rick Warren, Dr. Russell Moore, Ed Stetzer, David French, N.T. Wright, and many more. They all partnered, praised, and platformed a man who should be referred to as the Josef Mengele of this generation. Not unlike Francis Collins, the "Angel of Death" didn't perform the inhumane medical experiments himself. Mengele required other licensed medical professionals to perform the unenviable and grisly tasks of slicing open the bodies of his dead victims. Francis Collins is not a Christian. He is not "a man of integrity." He is not "a national treasure." He is not "committed to the human good." He is a supervillain, a swindler, and one of the architects of our current culture of death. The fact that our "theological betters" cannot or refuse to see that should tell you EVERYTHING you need to know about them.

As my friend Jon Harris of the *Conversations That Matter* podcast says, these kinds of men are not Christian leaders; they're institutional managers. Or to quote my friend Megan Basham, who broke the story that exposed these evangelical leaders' cooperation with evil, they are "evangelicals for hire." They are hirelings. They're the men whom Jesus warned us against because they do not care about the sheep. This egregious example is all the worse, for they are hirelings in the service of evil. Let me say it again: There is a reason why Rick Warren is invited to the World Economic Forum and Pastor Jack Hibbs is not. There is a reason why David French has a regular op-ed in *The New York Times* and Eric Metaxas does not. There is a reason why *The Washington Post* interviews Russell Moore for the "evangelical take" on current issues and not Voddie Baucham. The former are hirelings. The latter can't be bought.

I have spent a good amount of this chapter focused on the apparent schoolboy crush many of evangelicalism's elites have on Francis Collins. That's because it is a relatively recent and particularly egregious example, and it's one that perfectly displays the sycophantic urges of those who will not fight for biblical truth and a godly society but will instead dance like trained monkeys for the latest Leftist cause —as long as they can continue to have a seat at the cultural table. But even the table is a lie because those who pursue godlessness and an authoritarian state devoid of individual liberties grow tired of the Christian puppets they control.

In the fall of 2022, Eric Metaxas returned to my podcast, *The Seth Gruber Show*. We talked about the similarities between our current cultural moment and the situation facing pastors in Nazi Germany in the 1930s. Martin Niemöller was a Lutheran pastor who initially thought he could work with Hitler's regime. He understood the Nazi party was doing questionable things, but he held out hope that perhaps he could influence the direction. In a famous meeting with Hitler in the late 1930s, Niemöller finally saw the light. He went into the room filled with hope for a better Germany, but then Hitler told him, "You just worry about your sermons and let me worry about the Third Reich." In other words, "You stay in your theological lane and preach your little gospel messages, and I'll run the world. You will bow to the authority of the state and your Führer."

Those who bow to the powerful and well-positioned in the United

States today imagine that if they make nice, they'll be allowed to continue their ministries unabated. But progressives aren't interested in changing their religion, nor do they want Christian values to spread among the populace. They are fine entertaining those evangelical leaders who can speak to the rabble on their behalf, but they're no friends of the church.

Before our time was over, Metaxas shared about a Christian radio personality—he graciously did not provide his name—with whom he had connected at that year's convention of the National Religious Broadcasters Association. This fellow actually bragged about how he avoided certain hot-button issues on his show because, as he put it, staying clear of controversy would allow him to stay on the air for many, many years. However, no amount of appeasement will ever make the Christian faith safe if our nation continues on its current trajectory.[49]

Niemöller woke up after it was too late. Hitler's death cult had already taken over German society. There was no going back, no way to change course, no way to undo the damage that was being done. But until that moment in Hitler's office, he truly thought that if things ever got *really* bad—he didn't understand how bad they actually were at that point—there was still time to make a change in Germany. That's where many Christians are today. They imagine we can simply vote our way out of our progressive slide or, if given enough time, we can win people over simply by being nice. But we're too far gone for that. Of course, we should vote for our values and certainly, we should show people the love of Christ. But we must stand up and fight as well. We must oppose every wicked idea with kingdom resolve and every damnable lie with truth.

Now is not the time to avoid controversy. Like John the Baptist—a man about whom Jesus said, "Among those born of women there has not risen anyone greater" (Matthew 11:11b)—we must speak truth to power and proclaim what is just, right, and true. John wasn't rubbing elbows with Judea's elite. He wasn't invited to the best parties either. He was too busy honoring God to worry about any of that. We may end up in trouble, persecuted even, but we are no followers of Jesus if we compromise what we know to be true for the sake of comfort and respectability.

The truth is, what we're seeing today in the church is not normal. For much of the past 2,000 years, Christians have been at the forefront of social change, making this world a better place. Our situation may appear dark at the moment, but the arc of history is toward a world that looks more and more like Christ's kingdom. The idea that we are *Not in It to Win It*, as professional Scripture-twister Andy Stanley titled his 2022 book, is a complete and utter sham (just like the book). However, we must remember who we are and what God has called us to—and it is to that subject we turn next.

CHAPTER SEVEN
THE DIVINE TRAJECTORY OF GOD'S PEOPLE

"We shall have all eternity to celebrate the victories, but we have only the few hours before sunset in which to win them."

—Amy Carmichael

It was found in a forgotten corner of the temple of Yahweh, the holiest site on earth yet one that had been long neglected by the people of God. The workers were there to do some renovations to the building, but it was the nation itself that needed an overhaul. Amidst the dust and stone, far from the Asherah pole that was on full display in the temple, a scroll containing the very words of God was retrieved.

As far as noteworthy discoveries go, this was a big one. Hilkiah, the high priest, read the words on the scroll and then, with the urgency of his position, brought the book to Shaphan, the king's secretary. Shaphan, too, unrolled and read. He knew it needed to be brought to Josiah's attention at once.

King Josiah listened in stunned silence as Shaphan read the words of the Book of the Law aloud. Commandments and promises, blessings and curses—all of it rushed forward from the days of Moses to fill his chamber. When the secretary finished reading, Josiah dropped to his knees, tore his robes, and wept. Here he was, the leader of God's people, and he had failed to lead them according to the ways laid out by the Lord for his ancestors.

There could be no pleading ignorance; the Law should never have been neglected or forgotten in the first place. It wouldn't do to try and distance himself from his forebears either. That's not how a covenant with the Almighty works. The only thing Josiah could do was bring the people of Judah back into alignment with God's will for the nation—and he had no time to waste.

The people of Judah had all but abandoned the worship of Yahweh for the worship of other gods. They made sacrifices in the high places, they indulged male temple prostitutes, and they even burned their children as offerings to the dark gods. They bowed down before Baal, Asherah, and the sun, moon, and stars. They hosted mediums and spiritists in the land God had given to them. And they neglected the times, seasons, and festivals set by the Lord. In short, over the centuries, prodded and prompted by the rule of wicked kings, the people had become indistinguishable from their pagan neighbors—except for one thing: they may have embraced sin on a deeper level.

Josiah knew that too much time had passed already. He called the people of Judah to a sacred assembly and read the scroll that was found so everyone could hear the words of the Lord for themselves. Then, he pledged the nation to the covenant anew, and the people joined their voices in agreement.

Next, Josiah began the difficult work of cleansing the land. He removed the Asherah pole from the temple and had it burned and its ashes spread over the graves of the common people. He removed the dwellings in the temple courts where the male prostitutes lived. He executed the priests who led the people in the worship of false gods, and he tore down the high places where incense was burned and sacrifices were made. He destroyed altars throughout the land, and he desecrated Topheth, the shrine in the Hinnom Valley where parents murdered their children to curry favor with the demon gods.

Sadly, Josiah's reforms did not last for long. When he died, the people reverted to their old ways, neglecting the covenant with Yahweh and chasing after the promises of demons. God's judgment on the land, though postponed, was not revoked. Within a generation, Judah was trampled by the Babylonians, and God's people were hauled off into exile, just as the covenant had stipulated. Josiah's reign was an age of reform because Josiah served the living God:

> He did what was right in the eyes of the LORD and followed completely the ways of his father David, not turning aside to the right or to the left.... Neither before nor after Josiah was there a king like him who turned to the LORD as he did—with all his heart and with all his soul and with all his strength, in accordance with all the Law of Moses. (2 Kings 22:2; 23:25)

While other Old Testament kings followed in King David's footsteps, there were none who got the high praise Josiah did. Why? Because every time, they either stumbled toward the finish line, losing faith and compromising their commitment—I'm looking at you, Hezekiah—or they failed to tear down the high places, the sites where sacrifice and worship were offered to dark gods (see, for example, 1 Kings 22:43; 2 Kings 12:3; 15:4).

Josiah heard the words of the Book of the Law, and he was *all in*. There was no compromise within him, no desire to appease the influential leaders in Judah, no fear for his reputation, and no stomach for anything short of total dedication to the Lord. He was the king. God had made him the leader of the nation, and it fell on his shoulders to bring the culture and the government back into alignment with God's good ways. While Josiah's reforms might not have held together past his lifetime, he did the right thing for his generation. That's all any of us can do.

Looking back, it's easy to think of King Josiah as merely a bright twig on a particularly ugly family tree, but he's more than that. He's a model for us to follow. Today, just as it was back then, God's desire is for His people to stand up to evil, defend the defenseless, and push culture in a direction that honors Him. Yes, Josiah's dedication is unique among Old Testament kings, but it shouldn't be unique among God's people today.

Ever since Pentecost, Spirit-filled followers of Jesus have brought

Josiah-level dedication to their own cultures and spheres of influence. Many shifted their corner of the world toward the kingdom in ways that are still felt today. In the pages that follow, I'll highlight a few of these saints, otherwise ordinary people who took seriously God's command to love their neighbors. Like Josiah, they tore down the high places and desecrated the altars of child sacrifice. They stood when others bowed. They fought when others cowered in the corner. And they spoke the truth when others settled for being winsome.[1]

Vespers had ended, and although it was late in the evening, there was one more act of devotion Basil had to perform. With some deacons following close behind, he led the way to a pagan shrine in the city. Though Christianity had been recognized as an official religion throughout the Roman Empire some four decades prior, the evil of the darkest kind still held firm roots in various places. Caesarea in Cappadocia was one of them.

It's hard to imagine venerating such an abominable practice in stone, but there it was before his open eyes—a shrine to infanticide. The men could have circulated a petition in service of removing it from public view, or they could have written a strongly worded letter to the civil magistrates. But there are some things so wicked they cannot be tolerated. Under the night sky, with the moon and stars as their light, Basil and those deacons tore down the shrine, stone by stone, bit by bit, with their bare hands. It would no longer serve as a beacon for murder.

Basil of Caesarea was an influential church leader in the fourth century, but his influence far outlasted him. Having been born into a prominent and wealthy family, he could have chosen any career path. But he chose to follow God's calling into the ministry, and his assignment was to serve the people of Caesarea.

As soon as he arrived, he witnessed the plight of the sick and the poor in his new community, so he began administering the most potent form of medicine at his disposal—the Gospel of Jesus Christ. Basil is said to have conducted eighteen church services weekly and more in the days leading up to Christianity's high holy days of Easter and Christmas. But Basil did more than preach the good news of the kingdom; he also demonstrated the good news by promoting almsgiving in the church and by establishing the very first non-ambulatory hospital.

It was Basil's entrance into the healthcare arena that first brought him into conflict with the vile practitioners of abortion, infanticide, exposure, and abandonment in his community. Though Christianity was widely accepted, there were still large segments of the population who had yet to be evangelized, and the most disgusting elements of pagan culture persisted. In fact, to Basil's shock, killing children before and after birth by a variety of methods was still legal.

Basil discovered a guild of abortionists selling potions, devices, and surgical procedures to end the lives of unborn children. They would then sell the remains of the children they murdered to Egyptian cosmetologists, who would use the collagen from their bodies to produce various beauty creams.

Rather than seeing such a depraved and diabolical industry as a complicated issue that must be approached with nuance so as not to offend non-Christians, as some might today, Basil faced it head-on. He began preaching vehemently against the evils of abortion and infanticide, while he simultaneously taught the sanctity of life. He started a citywide education initiative to make sure everyone understood what was happening and how it was neither right nor good for society. He organized his church to care for families in need and women in crisis pregnancies.

Basil also used his powers of persuasion—and his family's substantial influence—to lobby for changes in the law. He used the authority of his office to denounce the abortionist guild as *anathema*, which excommunicated its members from the church. And he led protests against the Egyptian traders who purchased the bodies of dead babies.

It wasn't only the active killing of children that Basil fought against; there was also the ancient tradition of abandonment. In the Roman Empire, a child was not simply born into a family. Rather, the father had to decide to accept the child. Until he did that, the child had no rights or protections whatsoever. That meant a newborn baby could simply be abandoned and left for dead. It was neither a crime nor was there a social stigma attached to the practice. High places and walls were built outside of cities, especially for this purpose. A baby could be left cold and alone atop one of these monuments to die of exposure to the elements. It was such a shrine that Basil and his deacons toppled with their bare hands.

Basil was, in fact, so bold in his efforts that word reached the ears of Emperor Valentinian in Rome. Valentinian was so convinced by Basil's arguments against the murder of the unborn and the born alike that he issued a decree in 374, which ordered:

> All parents must support their children conceived; those who brutalize or abandon them should be subject to the full penalty prescribed by law.

With the stroke of his imperial pen, Valentinian made abortion, infanticide, abandonment, and exposure illegal. It was the first time in recorded human history that such a thing had happened. And it was Basil of Caesarea who had led the charge.

Basil died just four years later, at the age of fifty, but his influence lived on for centuries. Who knows how many millions of children were saved because of his heroic choice to stand up to wickedness? Not only did he save those lives, but he also altered the direction of an entire culture, revealing centuries-old practices to be despicable acts of evil that should be unthinkable for anyone with a conscience, let alone for those who bear the name of Christ.

Basil of Caesarea wasn't the first pro-life Christian, of course. The sanctity of life is a bedrock principle in the Jewish and Christian Scriptures, and all believers are called to protect the most vulnerable in our society. Given Basil's family connections, position, and prestige, he was well-suited to take a stand for life, especially given the relationship between the church and the state in his day. But long before Basil, courageous men and women fought against the tide of darkness in their spheres of influence. In the second century AD, Callixtus, also known as Callistus, was one such man.

Unlike Basil, Callixtus didn't come from wealth and privilege. He was a slave—and not a very good one. His master had taken up a collection for the poor and had entrusted Callixtus with it—and Callixtus lost the money. Some say he stole it, which may well be the case since he fled for his life. But he was soon arrested and returned to his master. A short while later, though, he was arrested again, this time for fighting in a synagogue. Apparently, he was trying to borrow money or collect old debts from some Jews, and his efforts ended in violence.

At this point, Callixtus was denounced by the church and sentenced to hard labor in the mines of Sardinia. He might have disappeared from history altogether if his story ended there, but due to the mercy of Hyacinthus, a Christian who had the ear of one of the emperor's mistresses, he was released and brought to the coast to recuperate from the toll the mines had taken on his body. He was even given a pension from the state.

Once Callixtus had recovered, he received a new commission and a new assignment from the church. Pope Zephyrinus made him a deacon and the caretaker of the first piece of real estate the church ever owned—a cemetery along the Appian Way. Because the site was church property, it was also a shelter for the poor and the hungry. Callixtus's job was to tend to the grounds and to the needs of those who sought refuge there.

His job became one big advertisement for the Christian faith. Christian burial practices demonstrated hope in a future resurrection. Pagans often burned their bodies, since they saw no future for them, but Christians planted their bodies in the ground like seeds waiting for spring. And when it came to Callixtus's care for the poor, it was an echo of God's love for lost sinners. Along the well-traveled Appian Way, people from nearly every walk of life came face to face with a gospel that challenged their assumptions about the nature of reality.

However, Callixtus's greatest impact on the Roman world of his day came when he decided to do something about a diabolical sin that plagued the culture. As you know from Basil of Caesarea's story, the abandonment of infants was an acceptable practice in the Roman Empire. There was no shame in leaving a newborn on a wall, a garbage heap, or even a dung pile.[2] Callixtus galvanized efforts to seek out and retrieve these tiny, struggling children from such places and place them into Christian homes. These "life watches" saved hundreds of boys and girls from certain death. Some years later, Callixtus was chosen to be bishop of Rome.

The air seemed thick with the Black Death, even if no infectious germs permeated the room. It was enough to know that nearly a quarter of the world's population had succumbed to the dreaded disease. Gerhard Groote knew he was living in dark days. Everywhere he looked, things only seemed to be growing darker.

In the fourteenth century, Western Europe was at a turning point. The Hundred Years War between England and France still raged, claiming thousands upon thousands of lives and bringing instability to both kingdoms. The rise of universities brought knowledge to many, but it also spread a certain form of scholastic humanism far and wide. Plus, Groote had experienced the debauchery that came with university life firsthand. Add to that the corruption that was visible in the church throughout Europe, and it appeared Christendom itself was ready to fall apart. It's no wonder Groote was ready to walk away from the Christian faith.

So, that's just what he did. Like the prodigal son in Jesus's story, Groote spent his time and his money on wild living, chasing after anything that might bring his life meaning. But nothing did. There was no pleasure, no experience, no philosophy that could bring him out of the darkness that seemed to surround him.

There was no reason to think things would get better anytime soon. And yet, Groote kept searching for something beyond the shadows, beyond the despair. And when nothing of this world proved to satisfy, he was met by the grace of God. He came home to faith and determined to live out his hope in ways that were conditioned on heaven's priorities, not those of the world around him.

As an ardent new convert in the midst of a church awash in promiscuous impiety, he lifted up an urgent prophetic voice against the evils of his day. He began to model a life of radical discipleship. And he attracted a strong following in his native Dutch lowlands.[3]

Groote's preaching was so effective that when people heard he had come to town, they would leave their businesses and even their meals to hear him preach. Churches were filled to overflowing when he took up the pulpit. He preached the Word of God and did not hold back, calling out the sins of the clergy as well as the sins of the laity. This, of course, enraged church officials, and the Bishop of Utrecht issued a decree prohibiting all but priests from preaching.

There was certainly a godly fire burning in the heart of Gerhard Groote, but when he died of the plague at the age of forty-four, he had not changed the world or the church. To most onlookers, he was a failure as a reformer. His voice did not change the culture; his light did not do nearly enough to pierce the darkness. The only revival lit was the one in his own heart. And yet, toward the end of Groote's life, he did something that made an impact many years later. He founded the society of the Brethren of the Common Life, which emphasized personal devotion to Jesus and the importance of living out religious convictions in daily life.

In Groote's lifetime, the Brethren was an incredibly small group. However, the schools that were founded as part of the society continued to grow in the decades following Groote's death. From those schools emerged nearly every single major figure of the Protestant Reformation, including Martin Luther, Ulrich Zwingli, John Calvin, Philip Melancthon, Martin Bucer, and Theodore Beza.

Until you picked up this book, you'd probably never heard the name Gerhard Groote. Even so, your life was affected by how he walked out his Christian faith. The man's devotion may have had little to no effect on his own generation, but he changed the world all the same. That's because Groote's eyes weren't fixed on his contemporaries or even on the generations to come. Instead, they were stayed upon King Jesus and His reign. He lived to serve the Lord, and it wasn't up to him to measure his success.

The devil doesn't have any new tricks. If you peruse history for very long, you'll see the same sins, the same lies, and the same culture of death rising again, even after previous generations did the hard work of suffocating the darkness with the light of Christ. Such was the world Vincent De Paul was born into.

In the mid-seventeenth century, the world had emerged from the Reformation, and modern nation-states were taking shape. Prosperity was transforming families and communities, bringing not only greater opportunity but also greater vice. Paganism was rising amid Christendom, and along with it, abortion and infanticide.

Vincent De Paul lived in this age of transition. Commissioned into the ministry at the age of twenty, De Paul had a special concern for the poor, and he reached out to peasants and slaves, orphans and convicts alike. His tactic was to mobilize and establish. He would mobilize disciples of Jesus for the task of caring for those whom society had forgotten, and he would establish institutions so the work could continue with or without him. He founded orphanages, hospitals, shelters, and poorhouses to prevent the least of these from falling through the cracks.

In 1652, De Paul became aware of an illegal abortion mill operating through midwives in the Parisian slums. These unborn children being snuffed out were the poorest of the poor and the lowest of the low, so he immediately began to fight on their behalf. He provided medical relief for the children who survived abortions and for the women who had them. But he didn't merely help with the physical needs.

De Paul took a page out of the books of those who came before him—men like Callixtus and Basil of Caesarea. He lifted his voice to the magistrates and leaders in the church, seeking civil justice for those who performed abortions as well as church discipline for those who participated in any part of the trade. At one point, De Paul even went undercover to expose the vile practice and raise awareness with the public.

Toward the end of his life, De Paul succeeded in changing attitudes toward abortion and infanticide. Although the spirit of the Enlightenment pushed back against traditional religious belief, De Paul had quickened the conscience of the body of Christ so that a strong pro-life movement continued long after his death. In fact, today there are members of the Society of Vincent De Paul still working to save the unborn.

Not everyone who enacts change is in a position to do so—at least not as society deems. Booker T. Washington was born in a hut in Franklin County, Virginia, to an enslaved mother; he never knew his white father. As a child, after he had moved with his family to West Virginia, he worked in a salt furnace from four until nine in the morning and afterward went to school. Then, he took on his second job in a coal mine.

It was at this second job that he overheard two other workers talking about a school for freed slaves back in Virginia. It was called the Hampton Institute, and it had been founded by Brigadier General Samuel Chapman, a Union leader of black troops during the Civil War. Washington knew school was for him, so, one day, at sixteen years of age, he began the five-hundred-mile trip on foot.

At Hampton, Washington excelled in his studies and soon stood out to Chapman. A few years after graduating, Chapman invited Washington to return as a teacher. Washington stayed at Hampton for a few years, but in 1881 he left to help found the Tuskegee Normal and Industrial Institute in Tuskegee, Alabama, known today as Tuskegee University. He was the school's first principal and remained at the helm until he died in 1915.

It might not sound all that impressive or world-changing to us today: Booker T. Washington established a school for African Americans in the deep South in the decades following the close of the Civil War. However, during his tenure as the head of school, Washington educated 1,500 students, brought on 200 faculty members, and oversaw an endowment of $2 million, ensuring the work he began would continue long after him.

Washington was a man of deep faith in Jesus Christ, and he believed the Lord had called him to improve the lives of African Americans through education. That was his singular focus. His attention to his mission won him the respect and admiration of millions, including US presidents. In fact, Booker T. Washington was the first African American invited to the White House.

Despite his acclaim, not everyone appreciated Washington's methods and singular focus. In a famous address given to a mostly white audience in September of 1895, he said:

> The wisest of my race understand that the agitation of questions of social equality is the extremest folly and that progress in the enjoyment of all the privileges that will come to us must be the result of severe and constant struggle rather than artificial forcing. The opportunity to earn a dollar in a factory just now is worth infinitely more than to spend a dollar in an opera house.[4]

Like the men of Issachar, Washington understood the times. It wasn't that he was opposed to integration on moral grounds; rather, it was that he knew forcing the issue would only create more problems for African Americans. Prejudice and injustice were widespread. Rather than confront them head-on, he decided to subvert them. He knew the best way to improve the conditions of the working poor within the black community was to make sure they had opportunities to earn money and provide for their families.

Washington had personally earned the respect of people who might otherwise have feared or hated him. And he did so not by fighting with the weapons of this world but by showing everyone—black and white—what it looks like to focus on loving one's neighbors.

This is in line with the apostle Paul's ethic when dealing with slavery. Slavery is evil and incompatible with the gospel. And yet, Paul didn't seek to overthrow the establishment. He didn't even seek to disqualify slaveowners from being members of their local church. When he encountered a runaway slave, he instructed him to return to his master. (See the book of Philemon.)

Wisdom requires we consider the cost before we take action. In everything, we are to seek greater human flourishing and a world that looks a lot more like the kingdom of God. Change does not happen overnight usually. Washington understood this, and he did his part in his generation.

The facility was not what Augustus St. Clair expected. It resembled an upscale spa more than an illicit abortion mill. He had heard rumors of back-alley procedures, unqualified medical personnel, and unsanitary conditions. What he found, however, were carefully appointed furnishings and décor, and staff that seemed every bit professional and qualified. The office itself was thoroughly clean, airy, and open. The sheer size of the place screamed profitability. Even so, this was not a cheerful space. The customers and patients wore shame and anxiety on their faces. St. Clair could almost see regret taking hold of these strangers as they waited to have their procedures.

St. Clair and a female friend posed as a couple looking to have an abortion. This gave them access to the doctors, nurses, and support staff, and the freedom to ask about pricing, procedures, and the sordid details of the illegal operation.

One of the customers whom St. Clair saw was a beautiful blonde woman of a slight build with striking features, about twenty years old. He would describe her in his article in *The New York Times*, detailing the illegal death trade taking place in the heart of New York City. (Believe it or not, in the 1870s, the Gray Lady sought to expose the abortion industry, not coddle it or defend it as it does today.) St. Clair was given the dangerous assignment of exposing the death merchants for what they were. Though the practice was illegal, abortionists acted with a great deal of impunity, being connected to corrupt politicians and gangsters alike. St. Clair knew he was putting his life in danger by agreeing to report on the trade.

When St. Clair's article appeared in the paper, it took up three columns. It was a gripping exposé that had the whole city and much of the country in shock. A few days after his report came out, the blonde woman he had mentioned in his piece was found dead, stuffed in a trunk, and left in the baggage room at a local train station. The autopsy determined the cause of death was a botched abortion.

An investigation soon uncovered everything—from the father of the deceased unborn child to the facility where the abortion had taken place to the doctor who performed the procedure. As it turned out, the abortionist was a prominent physician in the city with an office on Fifth Avenue. His name was Dr. Rosenzweig. Coincidentally, or really, providentially, St. Clair had interviewed him for his article. When asked about the remains—what happened to the unborn child's lifeless body after an abortion—here's what Dr. Rosenzweig said:

> "Don't worry about that, my dear sir. I will take care of the result. A newspaper bundle, a basket, a pail, a resort to the sewer, or the river at night? Who is the wiser?"[5]

Shortly after this point in St. Clair's interview with Rosenzweig, the wicked doctor began to get suspicious. Perhaps he had said too much, too freely. He wondered if the man and woman sitting across from him were, in fact, there to uncover the truth behind the clandestine abortion racket. When he became convinced, Rosenzweig retrieved a pistol and escorted St. Clair and his female accomplice off the premises at gunpoint.

If he hadn't known before, St. Clair now understood his reporting might land him in danger. It could even cost him his life. Nevertheless, his commitment to Christ and his Dutch Reformed upbringing would not permit him to turn aside from this narrow way. He wrote his article, knowing the consequences could be dire.

In God's hands, St. Clair's reporting became the catalyst for a revival of pro-life energy in the United States. Not just in New York but across the nation, faithful men and women began taking up the cause, investing their time and money into fighting the despicable practice of abortion.

Mental images of a young woman killed by her abortion and jammed into luggage horrified people of faith and character. Newspapers across the country began reporting in earnest on the issue. Even the American Medical Association, formed just a few years earlier, promoted the protection of the unborn as a medical necessity. Politicians and lawyers began taking up the cause as well. But most importantly, the church in America led the charge. D.L. Moody, the most famous and influential preacher of the day, wrote what became the prevailing sentiment in the evangelical church up to this present day, despite the inroads many progressives have attempted in recent years:

> Murder is, of course, heinous of its own accord. But the murder of a mother's own flesh within the womb is a crime against heaven that is the very essence of sin and inimicable with the Christian religion. Left alone, such a crime would sunder the whole fabric of our families, of our communities, of our churches, of our markets and industries, and finally of our nation.[6]

Amidst the ship's steady rise and fall, Anna Bowden could see land on the horizon. Finally, her long trip was nearly over. She would be in Conjeeveram soon, in the southeast of India. It would be home for the foreseeable future—not home because it would be comfortable, but home because it was where she belonged. It was where the Lord had called her to serve.

In truth, nothing could have been less comfortable for a lady who had grown up in London society. The land was filled with the darkness of paganism. The missionaries who served there were met with hostility from Hindu authorities. It wasn't going to be an easy life. But as Bowden wrote in her journal, "I know not the challenges that face me among peoples who live but for death. I do know, though, the grace of the Savior that has called me to die but for life."[7]

As a student at Henrietta Soltau's missionary training school in London, she had listened attentively to the itinerant evangelist Robert Campbell-Green describes the challenges of working in rural India. Campbell-Green described a harsh environment but one where the gospel was having a tremendous impact on the lives of the people. Though Bowden was only partway through her studies, she signed up for the mission in Conjeeveram. In just a few months, she found herself sailing halfway around the world to share the good news of Jesus Christ with people trapped in spiritual darkness.

Nothing could have prepared Bowden for what she found when she arrived at the mission. She had expected to be greeted by Campbell-Green and the other missionaries, but instead, she found the camp deserted with no signs as to what may have happened. Most people, when faced with such a development, would have packed up and headed home. But not Bowden. She determined to stay and do the work to which God had called her.

To her credit (and the Lord's faithfulness), within three months, she had the school and the clinic running again. And while the locals generally kept their distance from the strange (to them) Englishwoman, Bowden's warmth of personality drew in children and those deemed untouchable. She was making a real difference in the lives of the forgotten and the unseen.

Soon, however, Bowden found herself in a battle she felt she had no choice but to fight. A relatively new reform movement, designed to purify Hinduism from outside pollutants and restore the practice of the religion to its pagan roots, sought to ban proselytizing. This movement's proponents also restored several truly dreadful ancient practices, among them the sacrifice of widows on the funeral pyres of their husbands, the infanticide of girls, and ritual abortions through the use of certain potions. The year was AD 1893, but it might as well have been 1893 BC; the dark spiritual forces at work in that part of the world were just as brazen as their ancient-world counterparts.

Officially, British colonial policy was not to interfere with cultural beliefs and practices, no matter how opposed to traditional Christian values they were, and so many other missionaries simply allowed these practices to continue without a challenge to the local authorities. But

Bowden's conscience would not let her simply back down and allow the murder of the old and the young because such was a so-called cultural value.

Bowden was one person, but apparently, one person led by the Holy Spirit with a passionate drive to rescue the innocent can cause quite a stir. Bowden's influence was so oversized that one of the Hindu leaders of the region appealed to Queen Victoria's government to have the missionary silenced and restrained. Soon, an order came from London: Bowden was not to do anything that wasn't directly related to her missionary work. She responded by saying that saving lives and rescuing the oppressed was directly related to Christian relief work and evangelism. She would not stop—not one bit.

A short time later, the sound of an angry mob could be heard on the mission grounds. Soon after, the smell of smoke began to permeate the air. Buildings were being torched to the ground. But infinitely more horrible was what came next: the screams of young girls being raped by violent, twisted men filled with demonic hatred. In the attack, Bowden herself was killed. Her voice was silenced by the only thing that could silence her in this world—death. As she pledged, she gave her life for Christ and His work. Though to the world her death might have seemed senseless, she finished well for the kingdom.

As is often the case, the blood of a martyr sowed the fields for revival. Word of Bowden's death reached far and wide. Within India, missionary communities that had played it safe previously were emboldened and renewed their efforts. The result was the sort of fruit that hadn't been seen in a generation. Back in London, the magistrates faced new pressure, and soon official colonial policy was changed to recognize the sanctity of life in all places, regardless of the traditional culture.

Anna Bowden changed the world by her life and by her death because she knew the kingdom of God would have the final say. Though our circumstances may be quite different from Bowden's in rural India, we have the same choice before us. We can hide our lives in safety and security, or we can spend them on that which is eternal.

In December of 2023, a Baphomet display was placed in the rotunda of the Iowa State Capitol at the behest of the Satanic Temple of Iowa. For several days it stood there, ram's head and mirrors, candles and black robe, one of many "holiday displays" granted by lawmakers in the Hawkeye State.

Some argued that in a society where freedom of speech and freedom of religion are guaranteed rights, it was perfectly fine to showcase a pagan idol in the legislative house of the people of Iowa—especially if other religious groups got a turn. Others were simply disgusted at the promotion of evil on public display with the full blessing of state lawmakers. They were offended because God's word clearly tells us:

> Woe to those who call evil good and good evil, who put darkness for light and light for darkness, who put bitter for sweet and sweet for bitter. (Isaiah 5:20)

The statute of Baphomet stood there, mocking the Christian faith and all who practice it—that is, until Michael Cassidy of Mississippi entered the capitol building, grabbed the head of the idol, and smashed it on the floor. It was deemed "destroyed beyond repair"[8] by the Satanists, a fitting end to a statue honoring one whose destiny is eternal and unquenchable damnation.

When asked why he did it, Cassidy said the statue was blasphemous,[9] and he felt compelled to engage in an act of Christian civil disobedience.[10] It was an act for which he felt no shame. He didn't try to hide what he did, nor did he seek to run from the authorities. Instead, after destroying the evil totem, he sought out a security guard so he could turn himself in. He was given a citation for fourth-degree criminal mischief and released. The charge was later upgraded to third-degree criminal mischief, a felony classified under the state's hate crime laws.

This is where we are as a society. We're debating whether or not it's good to oppose Satan and his works. If there's ever been a time when the people of God need clarity of mind and a vision of the kingdom of God, this is it. Perhaps the most scandalous element of the whole

Baphomet-in-the-State-Capitol story is that the statue was allowed to stand for so long. Cassidy isn't a radical; he was just the first person to come along with enough common sense to do what needed to be done, the first person to concern himself with the Lord's honor.

In Numbers 25, we read about a man of similar disposition. Many Israelite men had been seduced by the women of Moab and were engaged in sexual immorality and idolatry. God told Moses the leaders of the people must be killed as a consequence (v. 4). A plague also broke out, killing 24,000 people (v. 9).

In the midst of this, a man named Phinehas saw an Israelite man bringing a Moabite woman into his tent. Phinehas didn't ask for permission or consult anyone concerning his plans; he simply got up, grabbed a spear, and followed the couple into the man's tent. Then he stabbed the man in the back, pushing the blade deeper and deeper until it came out the other side and continued into the woman's stomach. After that, the plague stopped.

> The LORD said to Moses, "Phinehas son of Eleazar, the son of Aaron, the priest, has turned my anger away from the Israelites. Since he was as zealous for my honor among them as I am, I did not put an end to them in my zeal. Therefore tell him I am making my covenant of peace with him." (Numbers 25:10–12)

History changes when people are zealous for the honor of God. Sometimes action requires everything a person has; other times it simply means speaking up. For every famous martyr or hero of the faith who acted to protect the innocent, there are 10,000 more who are unknown. We are moving toward the coming kingdom of God, day by day, year by year. Nothing can stop it. God has decreed it. But He also has decreed that it will be His people who change the world, one decision at a time.

We have not been given permission to be passive. We cannot afford to stand by while Marxists, progressives, and neo-pagans seek to drag the world backward into another dark age. We must stand and fight. We must be people who are zealous for the kingdom, men and women like those whose stories are included in the previous pages. In the next chapter, I will tell you about a young woman named Sophie Scholl, the resistance movement she began in Nazi Germany, and how we are continuing the fight today in the United States. It's now our opportunity to push history forward, closer to the kingdom of God.

CHAPTER EIGHT
THE WHITE ROSE RESISTANCE 1.0

"Who among us has any conception of the dimensions of shame that will befall us and our children when one day the veil has fallen from our eyes and the most horrible of crimes—crimes that infinitely outdistance every human measure—reach the light of day?"

—The White Rose Resistance

As she walked down the ordinarily pristine streets of Munich, she noticed a piece of paper on the ground, flitting in the wind. Curious, Sophie Scholl knelt to retrieve it. "A Leaflet of the White Rose," it was titled. She began to read and soon discovered it was part of an anti-Nazi campaign.

Two thoughts immediately entered young Sophie's mind. First, the sentiments the leaflet contained were the sort of thing that would land the writer or anyone caught distributing it in prison, facing a charge of treason. Second, what she was reading sounded like something her brother Hans would say.

As a young girl, Sophie joined the League of German Girls, and her brother Hans joined the Hitler Youth. Both Nazi youth groups had worked to sow the values of the party into their hearts and minds. But Sophie and Hans's parents were devout Christians, and they had opposed the regime from the start. As Sophie and Hans grew older, they saw the truth for themselves, and they too opposed the Nazi regime that had overtaken Germany.

Sophie was disgusted at the yellow stars the Jews were made to wear in public. She was incensed by the rumors and reports of concentration camps and gas chambers. Staring at that leaflet, Sophie Scholl wanted in. She wanted to join the White Rose Resistance, though she knew such a commitment might cost her her life. She also knew evil is powerless if good people are unafraid. At that moment, Sophie chose to not be afraid.

When Sophie did find the White Rose, she discovered she was right—her brother Hans was at the helm. Three other students from the University of Munich, Willi Graf, Christoph Probst, and Alexander Schmorell, and one professor, Kurt Huber, rounded out the group. At twenty-one, Sophie became their youngest member and the only female. But she was no junior member; she was fully committed to the cause.

From June 1942 until February 1943, the White Rose distributed leaflets throughout Germany, a feat that was tremendously difficult due to the rationing of paper, ink, and mailing supplies. However, Hans and the others found sympathizers and supporters near and far who helped them gather materials and who also served as distributors. Hans wrote most of the leaflets and typed them out. Then, using a mimeograph machine, the group would make thousands of copies to be mailed to their distributors, left in phone booths, and placed where students and professors would find them. They hoped that young people and academics would be quickened by what they had to know was evil. One of the leaflets read:

> But our present "state" is the dictatorship of evil. "Oh, we've known that for a long time," I hear you object, "and it isn't necessary to bring that to our attention again." But, I ask you, if you know that, why do you not rouse yourselves, why do you allow these men in power to rob you step by step, both

openly and in secret, of one of your rights after another, until one day nothing, nothing at all will be left but a mechanized state system presided over by criminals and drunkards?[1]

The White Rose knew they were facing the very destruction of their way of life—of everything they loved about their country and their freedoms. And the most frustrating part of it was that it seemed no one was willing to oppose the Reich. Fear kept people compliant, and that compliance only emboldened the monsters who sought to harm their countrymen.

In another leaflet—their third—the group promoted active resistance and gave specific examples:

> And now every resolute opponent of National Socialism must ask himself how he can fight against most effectively the present 'state', how we can inflict the most damaging blows.... We cannot provide each man with a blueprint for his acts; we can only make general suggestions, and he alone will find the best way to achieve them: *Sabotage* armament industries, *sabotage* every assembly, rally, ceremony, and organization sponsored by the National Socialist Party. Obstruct the smooth functioning of the war machine.... *Sabotage* all publications, all newspapers, that are in the pay of the "government" and that defend its ideology.... Try to convince all your acquaintances... of the senselessness of continuing, of the hopelessness of this war; of our spiritual and economic enslavement at the hands of the National Socialists; of the destruction of all moral and religious values; and urge them to adopt passive resistance![2]

While the Gestapo had been looking for the perpetrators of the White Rose leaflets for months, this third leaflet enraged officials, and their search intensified. At the same time, members of the White Rose grew emboldened in their efforts. They began experimenting with another form of expression—graffiti. In the dark of night, they painted anti-Nazi and anti-war slogans in public places throughout Munich.

For example, on the wall of the library at the university, they sprayed, "Down with Hitler!" in German.

In the beginning of 1943, the White Rose took things to the next level. They planned a massive leaflet distribution at the University of Munich. Hans and Sophie would take the lead to leave Christoph Probst out of it. They knew what they were about to do could result in their arrest, and Christoph was married with three children, one of whom had just been born. The stakes were higher for him. Besides, he had written the leaflet they would be circulating; that had been dangerous enough.

On February 18, 1943, with 1,700 copies of Christoph's leaflet stuffed in a suitcase, Hans and Sophie walked onto campus. They went while class was in session, so there would be fewer students and faculty walking the halls. They placed stacks of leaflets outside of every classroom. They wanted to make sure every student was confronted with the truth in the hopes that many would begin to resist.

Hans and Sophie might have delivered their leaflets and walked off campus with no one having known who was responsible for the paper trail of treason against the Third Reich. However, Sophie, ever the bold one, realized she had about a hundred copies of the leaflet left in her pocket, so at the last minute, she veered from the exit and up the stairs. Once on the third floor, Sophie took the stack of pamphlets and sent it flying off the balcony. The papers floated down to the atrium below in a storm of protest and youthful exuberance. It was a beautiful thing—but it also caught the attention of Jakob Schmid, a janitor at the university and a loyal supporter of the Nazi regime.

In sixty seconds, several things happened: the leaflets rained down onto the floor of the atrium, the bell rang, the halls began to fill with students, and Schmid raced up the stairs, weaving his way through those students, seeking the person responsible for the mess of anti-Socialist sentiment. Though Sophie and Hans ran, Schmid called for the Gestapo, and both were apprehended. The brother and sister might have been able to deny their way out of the allegations, but in Hans's pocket, the police found a paper with the handwritten text of the leaflet they had just distributed.

Of course, during their interrogations, Hans and Sophie refused to identify the other members of the White Rose. They had been caught, and they were willing to suffer the consequences for what they had done, but they saw no need to drag their friends and allies into the same trouble. However, the handwritten copy of the leaflet in Hans's pocket betrayed them. Before it was discovered, Hans had tried to tear it up and swallow the pieces of paper, but the officer arresting him was able to recover enough for the Gestapo to identify Christoph Probst as the writer of the material. He was arrested a short time later. Though Hans and Sophie had done their best to protect their friend, the husband and father who had so much to lose, they had failed.

Sophie's interrogator, Robert Mohr, chose her personally "intrigued by this young, innocent-looking woman who seemed utterly unintimidated as she stood among Gestapo officials in a building of barred windows and doors."[3] Taken with Sophie, Mohr tried to save her life by persuading her "to confess her sins and declare herself for National Socialism."[4] At the end of their seventeen-hour interrogation, in a final attempt to save her, Mohr "tried to explain the National Socialist worldview to her, to show her what Adolf Hitler had accomplished."[5] Sophie rejected these gestures and refused to bow to the Third Reich. She simply replied, "You're wrong. I would do it all over again—because I'm not wrong. You have the wrong worldview."[6] At this comment, Mohr ended the interrogation and sent Sophie back to her cell, where she would await her trial.

―――

A short distance from the University of Munich campus was a cold and imposing building that housed the *Volksgerichtshof*, the People's Court. On February 22, 1943, just four days after being arrested, Hans, Sophie, and Christoph were put on trial. The charge was treason.

The judge in the courtroom that day was Roland Freisler, a fervent Nazi who had earned a reputation for being especially harsh. In a last-ditch effort to try to save Christoph, Hans and Sophie confessed to the charges and took full responsibility for the work of the White Rose. But it didn't matter. Freisler pronounced the three of them guilty and sentenced them to death by beheading, a sentence to be carried out that very day. In defiance true to her nature, Sophie shouted to the judge, "Where we stand now, you will soon stand!"[7]

Friesler stared down at the three young people before him. It didn't make any sense to him. These twenty-somethings had all been raised in good German homes, had attended good German schools, and had been members of the Hitler Youth. How was it possible that they chose a path that led to treason against their nation? How could it be that they would stand here in the People's Court with their heads held high rather than begging for mercy? What had so radicalized them?

Sophie was just twenty-one years old, and yet she had learned to see past the veneer of this world. During the trial, she had said to Friesler, "Somebody, after all, had to make a start. What we wrote and said is also believed by many others. They just don't dare to express themselves as we did." Later on, before the sentence came down, she did not shake with fear, as many others would have. Instead, as though taunting Friesler, she said to him, "You know the war is lost. Why don't you have the courage to face it?"[8]

Sophie knew the Nazis could take her life, but they could not touch her soul. She knew, too, that in the end, the only kingdom left standing would be the kingdom of God. And everyone will appear before the judgment seat of the Lord. In her place and time, the Nazis held power over her. They could silence her by removing her head, but they would not have the final word.

Even during the era of the Third Reich, a German legal tradition continued—that of allowing the condemned to make a final statement to the world. As you can imagine, many facing severe sentences or death used this opportunity to plead for mercy or to show remorse before their accusers. But not Sophie Scholl. She used the minutes granted to her to make one last appeal to her fellow Germans gathered in the courtroom that day. She said:

> Time and time again one hears it said that since we have been put into a conflicting world, we have to adapt to it. Oddly, this completely un-Christian idea is most often espoused by so-

called Christians, of all people. How can we expect righteousness to prevail when there is hardly anyone who will give himself up to a righteous cause? I did the best that I could do for my nation. I therefore do not regret my conduct and will bear the consequences.[9]

By all accounts, Sophie Scholl lived out her final hours determined not to bend or break. On the back of her indictment papers, she scrawled the word *freedom*.[10] Even though she knew the Nazis were about to take her life, she had not allowed them to make her a slave. She remained free to the end. And as she saw it, her life was not being wasted; it was being spent for a noble and good purpose, one that her conscience would not allow her to abandon:

> The real damage is done by those millions who want to "survive." The honest men who just want to be left in peace. Those who don't want their little lives disturbed by anything bigger than themselves. Those with no sides and no causes. Those who won't take measure of their own strength, for fear of antagonizing their own weakness. Those who don't like to make waves—or enemies. Those for whom freedom, honour, truth, and principles are only literature. Those who live small, mate small, die small. It's the reductionist approach to life: if you keep it small, you'll keep it under control. If you don't make any noise, the bogeyman won't find you. But it's all an illusion, because they die too, those people who roll up their spirits into tiny little balls so as to be safe. Safe?! From what? Life is always on the edge of death; narrow streets lead to the same place as wide avenues, and a little candle burns itself out just like a flaming torch does. I choose my own way to burn.[11]

After Hans, Sophie, and Christoph were transported back to Stadelheim Prison, the guards decided to let Sophie and Hans have a few minutes with their parents—a special privilege normally withheld from the condemned. However, the guards had been so impressed by the bravery and resolve of the brother and sister that they granted them time to say goodbye. Earlier that day, during the trial, Robert and Magdalena Scholl tried to enter the courtroom. A guard stopped them, and Magdalena protested, "But I'm the mother of the accused." At that, the guard responded coldly, "You should have brought them up better." Undeterred, Robert Scholl pushed his way into the courtroom anyway. He was immediately seized, and they dragged him from the room as he proclaimed, "I'm here to defend my children!" The guards hauled Robert outside with a struggle, and everyone inside the courtroom could hear him shouting, "There is a higher court before which we all must stand," and as the doors closed, he added, "They will go down in history!"[12] That might have been the last time either Robert or Magdalena got a glimpse of Hans or Sophie but for the kindness of the prison guards. They were brought in one at a time, first Hans then Sophie.

Hans thanked his parents for loving him so well, and he asked them to give his final regards to many friends and family members, whom he named individually. As he spoke to his parents, he held back tears—his final gift to them was to spare them the pain of seeing him cry. He smiled at them one last time, and with his head held high he was escorted out of the room and back to his cell.

A few minutes later, a female prison guard brought Sophie into the room. "She looked thinner but rosier than usual, thought her mother." Sophie looked relaxed, committed to keeping it together in her final moments with her parents. Her mother, stumbling over her words said, "So you will never again set foot in our house." Sophie smiled. "Oh, what do these short years matter, mother?" she replied. Sophie, certain as ever said, "We took all the blame, for everything. That is bound to have its effect in time to come." Then Magdalena told her daughter, "Remember Jesus." "Yes," Sophie said, "but you, too." Like Hans before her, Sophie smiled as she looked at her parents for the last time. She was then brought back to her cell to await her execution. A few minutes later, Robert Mohr walked by the cell and noticed Sophie crying. She apologized and told him, "I have just said goodbye to my parents. You understand."[13] Sophie felt the weight of what was happening to her, of the price she was paying for her courage, but she refused to burden her mother and father with her pain.

For Christoph Probst, there was no final visit with family. No relatives came to see him during his brief prison stay. His wife Herta was still in the hospital recovering from delivering their third child, a daughter named Katja. Neither Herta nor anyone else in the family was even aware that Christoph had been arrested or that there was a trial or that he had been sentenced to die. The night before his execution, however, Christoph did receive one visitor—a Catholic priest who admitted him into the Roman Catholic Church *in articulo mortis* ("at the point of death"). "Now," he said, "my death will be easy and joyful."[14]

When the time came, Hans, Sophie, and Christoph were brought outside, one by one, to die for their crimes against the state. According to Sophie's cellmate, Else Gebel, before being led out to the yard to be executed, Sophie turned to her and said, "How can we expect righteousness to prevail when there's hardly anyone willing to give themselves up individually to a righteous cause? Such a fine sunny day, and I have to go now."

By custom, the executioner, Dr. Walter Roemer, asked each one as they faced the guillotine if they had any final words to speak before they departed this world. Christoph Probst is reported to have said, "I didn't know dying could be so easy." Under the blade, Hans shouted, "Freedom!" And Sophie, as defiant as ever—and as though she were continuing the thought she had begun in her cell when speaking to Else—said, "The sun still shines." One observer remarked that she walked to her death "without turning a hair, without flinching."[15]

Even in her final moments, Sophie's spirit rang out a note of hope and optimism. She truly believed the work of the White Rose would continue as people became inspired by their example. She had told Else, "What does my death matter if through us thousands of people are awakened and stirred to action?"[16] The only thing was that the deaths of Hans and Sophie and Christoph and the other members of the White Rose, who were all eventually arrested, tried, and executed, didn't fan the flames of resistance in Germany. There was no great wave of young people willing to fight the Nazi regime, and no movement within the church to speak out against the crimes being committed. The White Rose Resistance died with them. Heinrich Himmler even "made the decisions on how the proceedings would play out." Afraid that "public executions might be provocative and lead to further demonstrations," Himmler insisted they be killed "secretly and quickly" as a warning to students "to keep away from the fires of resistance."[17]

Perhaps if Sophie, Hans, and the others had lived just a while longer, their impact could have been multiplied. But their work throughout Germany had not gone unnoticed. Hans and Willi Graf had been in contact with Falk Harnack, a screenwriter and a member of the German Resistance movement. Hans was to meet with Harnack again in Berlin on February 25 so arrangements could be made to meet with Harnack's cousin and fellow Resistance member Dietrich Bonhoeffer.[18] But no meeting was held. Though Harnack waited at the agreed-upon time and location, the swiftness of Nazi "justice" saw to it that Hans had already been dead for three days.[19]

Not too long ago, I got the chance to visit Munich. While I was there, I wandered through the graveyard adjacent to Stadelheim Prison for a few minutes, and I found the graves of Sophie, Hans, and Christoph. They're next to one another, in a line, side by side even in death. The headstones themselves tell little of their story; they're just like the hundreds of others in that sad place—weathered and drab. In that graveyard, there's no celebration of their shared spirit, no monument to their courage. If you didn't know their names, you'd walk right past them.

However, in Germany today, lots of people know their names. Streets and buildings are named after members of the White Rose. They're considered national heroes, despite their humble resting places. In a country where citizens are eager to distance themselves from the frightful legacy of Adolf Hitler, the Scholls are an example of what every German should strive to be.

Sadly, in their generation, Hans and Sophie Scholl did not inspire widespread resistance to Hitler and his Nazi regime. They did not become martyrs who, by dying, rallied the multitudes to their cause. Sophie's hope that thousands would be stirred to action by their deaths did not materialize. They died and were buried, and the White Rose was buried with them. But here's the thing about roses: even though rose blossoms may perish in the fall, they reappear in the spring.

Before I decided to form a non-profit to combat the pervasive poison of the abortion industry in America, I read a biography about Hans and Sophie Scholl written by their sister Inge Scholl. (I figured if I were going to read a biography about them, it made sense to get as close to their lives as possible, and a book by their sibling fit the bill.) Even though the Scholls were resisting a different brand of evil—the extermination of the Jews and the destruction and subjugation of the untermenschen (subhumans)—I could see our battles were the same. It's for that reason that I decided to call our organization The White Rose Resistance. Our mission is to continue the work of Hans and Sophie Scholl—to awaken thousands—nay, millions—and stir them into action.

Once a society decides some segment of the population is no longer fully human, the evil will only steamroll until more and more groups are added to the list of undesirables. In recent history, it was the blacks, then the Jews, and then the unborn. At various times, it's been the disabled, the poor, and the addicted. No matter who it is at any given moment, if it's not resisted, eventually the powerful will come for everyone who is not essential to their power. Those who call themselves Christians and provide cover for progressivism's destructive path through our society believe that by serving their wicked masters they will somehow escape the fate of those who are being silenced and those who are being murdered in the womb. But eventually, they too will be opposed and condemned. There is no safety for anyone when evil is allowed to thrive unopposed.

Many of us want to look back on Germany during World War II and comfort ourselves with the thought that we would have opposed Hitler. The evil was so blatant, so palpable, so entrenched in everyday life that we would have stood strong against it. The truth is, the evil in

America in our day is just as blatant, just as palpable, and just as entrenched in our everyday lives, yet most of the church is asleep. We can't imagine there will be consequences for our silence.

It's true that Hitler's brand of satanic assault on his nation and all of Western Europe came at a fast pace. In some ways, his speed made it safer. It was easier to identify what his aims really were. But speed is not the only measure of a thing. Margaret Sanger was America's eugenics-crazed progressive monster, and in many corners of our nation, she is praised as a hero of feminism. Her burn was slower, but she was no less evil than Hitler—and measured in lives lost, she was far more deadly in her designs. Not by coincidence, in 1942, Sanger changed the name of her American Birth Control League to Planned Parenthood Federation of America. The organization's original name was strongly identified with the eugenics movement, and as the world was learning more and more about Hitler's crimes, Sanger knew distancing herself from the Nazis would be good for branding. She saw Hitler's mistake—moving too fast. Truly changing a culture must come by small steps.

A counterrevolution, on the other hand, takes all kinds. We need to take the small steps, the seemingly insignificant duties of tending to family and community. But we also need to step out in boldness, unafraid of what today's Gestapo might do to us. We need stubborn and courageous people like Sophie Scholl, men and women who will stare down evil and choose their own way to burn.

CHAPTER NINE
SAVED BUT NOT SALTY

"In keeping silent about evil, and burying it so deep within us that no sign of it appears on the surface, we are implanting it and it will rise up a thousand fold in the future."

—Aleksandr Solzhenitsyn

In January of 2023, I was in Washington, DC, just before the annual March for Life rally was set to commence. Because I was there early, I decided to scope out the disciples of Molech and the Baal worshipers, who would inevitably be waiting along the designated route with their rainbow flags, their "My Name Is Legion" T-shirts, and their homemade signs giving voice to their support of legalized baby slaughter.

As I roamed among the clusters of lost souls, wondering at the depravity that could make someone fight for the right to kill the most vulnerable members of our society, something caught my eye. On the side of a cart filled with signs and flags that said things like "F--- Off, Bigots" and "Keep Your Religion Out of My Vagina," there was another sign. Its message was "No Gods, No Masters," precisely what Margaret Sanger had blasted across the masthead of her first magazine,

The Woman Rebel, in 1914. Here I was, 109 years removed from those wicked beginnings, and the seed Sanger planted in American soil was still producing its poisonous fruit, still spreading through culture like a disease bred in Wuhan.

I don't know if the vile crew who displayed that sign knew its origins. Maybe they did. Maybe they knew all about Sanger and her disdain for the handicapped and the disabled, for the poor and the addicted and the "racially inferior." Maybe they knew about her prominent place at the heart of the international eugenics movement. Maybe they knew about her connections to Nazis and Nazi sympathizers. Maybe they knew and were in full agreement with Sanger's mission. But maybe they didn't know. It wouldn't make much of a difference to me. That "No Gods, No Masters" sign wasn't there by accident. Its presence was merely evidence that the spiritual force that has been assaulting our culture since Sanger's day—and even before—is still prowling around like a lion, looking for those he might destroy. It's evidence that the battle is, above all else, a spiritual one. Baal, Asherah, and Molech are still active, and God's people have not been given the choice to stand idly by and do nothing while their bloodlust continues.

Doing nothing was kind of Lot's thing. It's not that he was lazy or afraid of doing hard work. Everything we know about him from the book of Genesis tells us otherwise. Rather, it's that he was careful to avoid saying or doing anything that might compromise the lifestyle he had grown to love.

You may recall that Lot was Abraham's nephew and traveled to Canaan from the east with his uncle. For a while, Lot's family and Abraham's family lived and worked near one another, but when their respective herdsmen began arguing over grazing land, Lot moved his tents close to the city of Sodom. He didn't stay outside of the city for long though. After a season, Lot and his family moved within the gates of the city, and Lot became a respected member of the community. Of course, Lot didn't participate in the grotesque sins of the city. The New Testament tells us Lot was "a righteous man" (2 Peter 2:7).

Lot was the Christian influencer of his day. We're told that when angels arrived at the city gate, Lot was there to meet them. In the ancient Near East, the city gate was a meeting place for the elders of the city. Only a prominent citizen—someone well-regarded in the community—would have been given the privilege of manning the gate to welcome travelers. If Lot were around today, he'd be the sort of "righteous man" invited onto the Sunday morning talk shows to offer a faith perspective. He'd be a conservative Christian voice who might be invited to have his own op-ed in *The New York Times*.

So, these two angels come to the city gate, and Lot invites them into his home to be his guests. Remember, he's a righteous man. This is the kind of thing a righteous man does. He's warm and hospitable; he takes care of strangers. But listen to what happens next:

> Before they had gone to bed, all the men from every part of the city of Sodom—both young and old—surrounded the house. They called to Lot, "Where are the men who came to you tonight? Bring them out to us so that we can have sex with them." (Genesis 19:4–5)

The young and old from every part of the city came. Doesn't that feel like America today? Every part of culture descending upon the righteous, upon the remnant, upon the church—demanding not just tolerance or acceptance or even celebration, but that believers participate in their sin. They're shouting, "Bring those men out here so we can have sex with them!" Only, the visitors weren't men; they were angels. The townspeople wanted to bang angels. Is it any wonder God had decided to torch Sodom?

How Lot responds tells us a tremendous amount about his convictions. First, he addresses the sex-crazed mob and says, "No, my friends" (Genesis 19:7a). Let's stop there for a minute. The Hebrew word translated as *friends* in the NIV means "brothers." *They're not your brothers, Lot!* But isn't this what Big Eva types do today? They want to buddy up with the world. They try to lick up some of the crumbs of secular humanism falling from the table. They want to play nice so nothing happens to their 501(c)(3)s, their book deals, or their speaking schedules.

Facing the crowd of angry, lustful Sodomites, Lot then says, "Don't do this wicked thing" (v. 7b). He calls their actions *wicked*. He's willing to lob out some truth. He's even willing to criticize and critique the spirit of the age. Boy, do we have a lot of Christian pastors, podcasters, influencers, and authors today who are willing to criticize and critique the spirit of the age, to call out the culture of death—at least to a certain extent. But here's the problem with these men and women. Just like Lot, when evil is at their front door, they fold like a cheap suit. Lot is willing to appease his "brothers" by offering up his family. "Look, I have two daughters who have never slept with a man. Let me bring them out to you, and you can do what you like with them" (Genesis 19:8a).

"Please rape my daughters!" That's what Lot was willing to offer to keep his position, his comfort, his seat at the table. The testing point of every person is their ability and willingness to defend the least of these, particularly their own children. Evil wasn't just something *out there*—in the distant future, something hypothetical to speak against. It was staring him in the face. But because he had cozied up with the culture for so long, when the moment came for Lot to stand and fight, he offered up his children on a silver platter. Are Christian influencers today any different when they hand the culture over to those who hate the church? To those who hate them and their children? They imagine the evil will have to be dealt with by some future generation, but it's here now, standing on their doorstep of the American church, demanding that we participate in wickedness—and these cowards are holding the door open, saying, "I've got some daughters you might be interested in."

I'm going to have to say this again because it's easy to forget: Lot was a righteous man. He was saved. God rescued him from the destruction that came upon Sodom and Gomorrah. If you know this story, you know that when his family fled the city, "Lot's wife looked back, and she became a pillar of salt" (Genesis 19:26). Lot was supposed to be salt in the city of Sodom. He was supposed to be a preservative in a rotting society. But he failed to live up to his calling. He couldn't even be salt in his own home. He failed to protect his bride, so she allowed her heart to become attached to the vile city where they had built a life. In the end, she became in death what he should have been in life—a pillar of salt.

Lot was saved, but he wasn't salty. And what did Jesus say about salt that's lost its saltiness? "But if the salt loses its saltiness, how can it be made salty again? It is no longer good for anything, except to be thrown out and trampled underfoot" (Matthew 5:13b). Have you ever wondered why it often feels like the American church is being trampled? Is it because we've lost our saltiness and we've been thrown underfoot? Maybe that's why it feels like we're on the losing end of a stampede.

The culture of death is at the front door of our churches, but let me be clear about something: It's not about you. It's not about your gun rights or your right to free speech or free trade or any of that. Yes, I care about those issues, but this isn't about self-preservation. You have an obligation to act because of the next generation. You have a responsibility to care for the least of these.

As we have seen time and time again, evil men and women are often more zealous for—and unyielding with—their ideology than most Christians are zealous for pure and undefiled religion. You can be saved but not salty.

———

A safe Christian life without action is no life at all. It is a long, slow death—nothing more. In fact, we willingly abandon the greatest adventure we could ever know—being used by God. C. S. Lewis, the brilliant thinker that he was, tried to warn us about this in his book *The Screwtape Letters*. Consider the advice senior demon Screwtape offers his young protégé, Wormwood:

> No amount of piety in his imagination and affections will harm us if we can keep it out of his will. As one of the humans has said, active habits are strengthened by repetition but

passive ones are weakened. The more often he feels without acting, the less he will ever be able to act, and, in the long run, the less he will be able to feel.[1]

The enemy's strategy has always been to neutralize God's people—to make them talkers and not doers, to get them so comfortable in this world that they forget they're supposed to live for another. Elsewhere, Lewis wrote, "Courage is not simply one of the virtues but the form of every virtue at the testing point, which means at the point of highest reality."[2] In other words, faith without works, piety without action, is dead. Jesus's half-brother James had something to say on the subject:

> Do not merely listen to the word, and so deceive yourselves. Do what it says. Anyone who listens to the word but does not do what it says is like someone who looks at his face in a mirror and, after looking at himself, goes away and immediately forgets what he looks like. (James 1:22–24)

In other words, if we know the truth and don't act on it, we demonstrate we never really took hold of the truth in the first place. Remember Martin Niemöller? He was the Lutheran pastor who thought the best strategy for the church in Germany was to support Hitler's regime while still preaching the gospel from the pulpit. When he attempted to counsel Hitler, the Führer told him, "You just worry about your sermons and let me worry about the Third Reich." After that, he knew he'd made a terrible mistake. He knew he should have resisted the evil he had witnessed. But it was too late by that point. There was little that could be done. The Reich's hold on the culture was secure. He had missed his opportunity to be the man God had called him to be. This was the same Martin Niemöller who, years later, filled with anguish over his failure, wrote:

> First they came for the socialists, and I did not speak out—
> Because I was not a socialist.

Then they came for the trade unionists, and I did not speak out—
> Because I was not a trade unionist.

Then they came for the Jews, and I did not speak out—
> Because I was not a Jew.

Then they came for me—and there was no one left to speak for me.[3]

Those lines now adorn the entrance to the United States Holocaust Memorial Museum in Washington, DC, warning us all to be vigilant against the slow but sudden death that comes through accommodation. What Niemöller learned the hard way is that confession without resistance is not enough. Evil doesn't care if Christians confess the truth, so long as they don't act on it. Dietrich Bonhoeffer tried to warn men like Niemöller, but far too few listened. Contemplating his good friend Bonhoeffer's legacy, Eberhard Bethge wrote:

> Bonhoeffer introduced us in 1935 to the problem of what we today call political resistance. The levels of confession and of resistance could no longer be kept neatly apart. The escalating persecution of the Jews generated an increasingly intolerable situation, especially for Bonhoeffer himself. We now realized that mere confession, no matter how courageous, inescapably meant complicity with the murderers, even though there would always be new acts of refusing to be co-opted and even though we could preach "Christ alone" Sunday after Sunday. During the whole time the Nazi state never considered it necessary to prohibit such preaching. Why should it? Thus we were approaching the borderline between confession and resistance; and if we did not cross this border, our confession was going to be no better than cooperation with the criminals. And so it became clear where the problem lay for the Confessing Church: we were resisting by way of confession, but we were not confessing by way of resistance.[4]

Crossing over from confession to resistance is difficult, and in the beginning, otherwise, good men fool themselves into believing it's not strictly necessary. That's because cultural change is most often gradual, then sudden. Evil progresses slowly over time, but then it seems to come crashing down all at once so that what was unthinkable becomes the new standard. In the United States, we have witnessed this phenomenon in the last few decades concerning abortion. In 2008, Hillary Clinton famously said abortion should be "safe, legal, and rare." Not a new concept, she picked it up verbatim from her husband's campaigns in the 1990s.[5] The idea was that we all agree abortions are not good; the only question was, "Should they be legal?" A decade later, however, actual Democrat policies made it clear most progressives don't believe abortion should be rare or limited in any way.

In 2019, Virginia Governor Ralph Northam's representative Kathy Tran proposed a new reproductive health act to codify abortion through birth and remove abortion from the penal code. A judge forced her to admit that her bill would allow a woman who is dilating to request an abortion. Northam was asked about this radical bill on a radio show and what would happen to a baby who survived a botched abortion. He said, "We'd make the baby comfortable. We'd resuscitate the baby if that's what the mother wanted. And then the mother and the doctor would have a conversation." This led Senator Ben Sasse from Nebraska to propose the Born-Alive Abortion Survivors Protection Act (BAASPA), which did nothing to prohibit killing children in the womb. Nancy Pelosi and the Dems have vetoed and blocked that bill over ninety times.

We are now at fourth trimester abortions. California proved this in 2022 with Prop 1 and AB 2223, which prevented investigations into the deaths of babies due to abortion, miscarriage, or perinatal deaths. (*Perinatal* refers to children up to twenty-eight days after birth.) "Safe, legal, and rare" moved to infanticide far too quickly.

In 2020, one of the first actions of the Biden administration was to drop a lawsuit against a Vermont hospital, originally brought under Trump's Office of Civil Rights in the Department of Health and Human Services. The lawsuit was filed by a nurse who was coerced into assisting with an abortion upon threat of career termination. It was one of the clearest-cut cases of conscience violations in American history, and the Biden administration moved quickly to drop the lawsuit. What were they communicating? "You will kill babies, or else!"

A year later, Judicial Watch caught scientists at the University of Pittsburgh performing late-term abortions and scalping the heads of those recently murdered children—with funding from the NIH and NIAID (National Institute of Allergy and Infectious Diseases. These butchers then grafted those scalps subcutaneously onto lab rats, who would then begin growing the human hair that should have grown on the heads of those babies. In hell, Mengele blushed.

In 2022, the American Congress of Obstetricians and Gynecologists (ACOG) threatened to remove medical licenses from doctors who share "misinformation" on COVID and "reproductive healthcare." The lying ACOG, which has buried data on the RU-486 pill and the impact of abortion on mental health, preterm labor, breast cancer, and suicidal tendencies, is committed to silencing those who do not agree with their positions. And if you are a pro-life OB-GYN, you can kiss your career goodbye.[6]

That same year, after the overturning of *Roe v. Wade*, two pro-abortion domestic terrorist groups—Ruth Sent Us and Jane's Revenge—began firebombing, vandalizing, and attacking pro-life pregnancy centers and pro-life ministries, spray painting their buildings in blood-colored paint with the message, "If abortions aren't safe, then you aren't either." Merrick Garland and the Biden DOJ and DHS have shown zero interest in finding and arresting these domestic terrorists because, apparently, attacking pro-lifers is a special calling on Merrick Garland's life.

Near the end of 2022, Merrick Garland and the FBI began arresting pro-life sidewalk counselors. Starting with Mark Houck and proceeding with at least ten others, the FBI arrived at their homes, fully armed and unannounced, to take pro-life sidewalk counselors away in handcuffs and ankle cuffs for allegedly violating the Freedom of Access to Clinic Entrances Act (FACE). Most of these individuals were returned home the same afternoon. It turns out that, at least for now, Garland cannot easily prosecute pro-abortion domestic terrorists because he is himself a domestic terrorist.

Progressive social change always moves from tolerance to acceptance to celebration to participation. With abortion, they said, "We agree that abortion is a tragedy, but it needs to be made legal in the cases of horrific circumstances, just **tolerate** it." Then it became, "Actually, we want to make abortion legal through the point of birth. Not everyone shares your Christian belief that human life begins at conception. Why should your religious beliefs be imposed on the entire country? So just **accept** it." After that, it was, "We want to shout about our abortions. We're going to say that without this basic right, women can't be free. We want abortion on demand and without apology! Shout your abortion! Just **celebrate** it." Now, we're in the final phase. "We want to force Americans to fund abortions with their tax dollars. We want pro-life OB-GYNs who share abortion 'misinformation' to lose their medical licenses. We want pro-life nurses to be coerced into assisting and performing abortions upon threat of career termination. We want twelve-year-olds in California to be able to obtain an abortion without parental consent or knowledge and to be able to charge the abortion to their parents' insurance plans. And we want religious institutions to be forced into covering abortions with their healthcare plans too! Just **participate** in our agenda!"

Whenever conservative Christians give an inch, the wicked take a mile. As my friend Pastor Rob McCoy has said, "Tyranny is achieved by incremental steps by good people submitting to systematic control."[7]

For now, the FBI isn't banging down the doors of men like Russell Moore, David French, and Ed Stetzer, but if nothing changes, the Left will come for them as well. No amount of brown-nosing or bootlicking will satisfy the architects of the culture of death. They are not interested in preserving the church in any form—even the weak and impotent faith of men like Moore and French. No matter how many impressive parties they attend or how many bylines they receive in *The Atlantic*, so long as they continue to profess Christian faith and speak a modicum of truth, they will eventually find themselves in the crosshairs of progressive militants. Once again, remember what happened with Lot. The men gathered at his door didn't accept Lot's perverse offer of his virgin daughters. "'Get out of our way,' they replied. 'This fellow came here as a foreigner, and now he wants to play the judge! We'll treat you worse than them'" (Genesis 19:9a). In the end, they will come for anyone who bears the name of Jesus.

In the summer of 2023, the Washington DC-based Dupont Clinic made plans to open a new location in Beverly Hills. The word *clinic* in their name is a bit misleading. Rather than being some drab and serious medical clinic, Dupont is a full-blown luxury spa that aggressively promotes and conducts abortion up through the third trimester. Why merely kill your child when you can kill your child at a lavish resort, complete with aromatherapy sessions and a massage parlor? When Proposition 1 passed in California, DuPont saw it as an opportunity to expand its all-trimester murder mill to a new part of the country.

When I found out about the planned second location, I decided something had to be done. My non-profit, the White Rose Resistance, partnered with the group Survivors of the Abortion Holocaust. We decided we would go out and stage a very peaceful protest in front of the building where DuPont was getting ready to set up shop. My friend Pastor Jack Hibbs invited believers across southern California to join us. All told, about a thousand people showed up. I spoke along with some brave pastors and pro-life leaders. We worshiped together, and we made our opposition clear. I want to repeat: we had only a thousand people in one of the most church-saturated areas of America. We sang songs. There were no riots. There was no looting. Nothing was set on fire. There was no violence at all. All we did was show up and shine a spotlight on the vile butchery that was about to descend on Southern California.

And do you know what happened? During the event, one of the organizers received an email from a lawyer representing the building's owner. The message said the owner had decided to rescind the lease agreement with DuPont; they would not be operating in his building.

I've seen it happen time and time again. On so many occasions, all it takes to combat evil effectively is to show up and speak. Too often we fool ourselves into believing there's little we can do to affect change. That's simply not true. Sometimes all it takes to push back evil is to stare it square in the face and say, "No more."

Facing down sin peddlers and death merchants is part of our calling in Christ. There is no version of Christianity where some people have been chosen to sit on the sidelines. In describing the church, Jesus said, "The gates of Hades will not overcome it" (Matthew 16:18b). He was speaking of an attack on hell, a forward assault. There was no mention of retreat or merely holding territory. We are meant to shatter the darkness, not cower from it in some self-serving holy huddle. The Christian men and women down through the centuries who shaped history by their actions went on the offense. None of them—not one—played it safe.

Back to Lot for a moment. He was a righteous man. Apparently, we're going to meet him in heaven. But what story is he going to tell at the marriage supper of the Lamb? I'll tell you what it will be. He'll say, "I gave my daughters to be raped by a mob, and God forgave me. By grace and grace alone." What will your story be on that day, when you're standing beside people like Dietrich Bonhoeffer and Hans and Sophie Scholl? When you run into Augustus St. Clair or Callixtus or Anna Bowden? Or what about the millions of anonymous sidewalk counselors and prayer warriors who fought to keep innocent children from being butchered? History has not recorded their names, but Jesus knows each one. They will have more jewels in their crowns than most of us. What will your story be at the marriage supper of the Lamb? What will you say you did when evil came to your front door?

You can be saved but not salty. You can make it into the kingdom by the hair on your bum. Don't believe me? The Bible says there will be some who are saved "but only as through fire" (1 Corinthians 3:15b ESV). That means they're getting singed on their way into glory. That's a lot of us in the American church. We have been overtaken by the spirit of Lot. Far too many pastors and leaders and comfortable Christians are offering up the next generation to the sexualized, demonically-inspired culture of death, all so this life might be a little more comfortable, so they can keep their place at the table of Sodom. But that's not how followers of Christ have been called to live.

In an earlier chapter, I briefly recounted part of Gideon's story from the book of Judges. Gideon obeyed God and destroyed the altars to Baal and Asherah. It made him wildly unpopular with his neighbors. But it was the right thing to do. And it was the beginning of a cultural shift in his generation.

The American church is filled with men and women intoxicated by the spirit of Lot, but what we need are those who will rise with the spirit of Gideon and tear down a few of the altars to our current death cult. Chesterton once said, "We are perpetually being told that what is wanted is a strong man who will do things. What is really wanted is a strong man who will undo things; and that will be the real test of strength."[8] That's Gideon. That's who we need for this hour. The time for welcoming evil to rape our daughters is over.

AFTERWORD

Did this book disturb you? Anger you? Inspire you? Good! That's why I wrote it. So, what's next? If you're tired of a boring and sleepy Christianity and you want to make a difference in our wicked culture, you're at the right place.

The White Rose Resistance is not just an organization; it's a movement. Launched immediately following the overturning of *Roe v. Wade*, The White Rose Resistance was my response. An unapologetically Christian organization, I understand that unless the church in America wakes up and engages the culture of death with the same fervor that the secular Left has for preserving that wicked culture, nothing will change.

It's time to take action! You can be a part of the fastest-growing pro-life organization in America and help rebuild Christian resistance.

Here's your marching orders:

1. Become an ally of The White Rose Resistance to receive access to the digital community where you'll be equipped with courses, curriculum, and live calls with Seth. And connect with like-minded individuals committed to rebuilding a culture of life. You'll even receive a BATTLE BOX so you're ready for the fight.

2. Host a screening of *The 1916 Project* documentary at your church.
3. Book a White Rose Resistance speaker to speak at your church or school.
4. Join or launch a White Rose Resistance chapter in your city.

We are rebuilding The White Rose Resistance for this generation to prick the conscience of our culture and awaken the church to action. And we need your help!

Scan the QR code or visit www.thewhiterose.life for more information.

NOTES

1. WHITEWASHING THE WITCH

1. Planned Parenthood of Greater New York, "Planned Parenthood of Greater New York Announces Intent to Remove Margaret Sanger's Name from NYC Health Center," news release, July 21, 2020, https://www.plannedparenthood.org/planned-parenthood-greater-new-york/about/news/planned-parenthood-of-greater-new-york-announces-intent-to-remove-margaret-sangers-name-from-nyc-health-center.
2. Margaret Sanger, "Letter from Margaret Sanger to Dr. C. J. Gamble," Genius, Accessed June 19, 2023, https://genius.com/Margaret-sanger-letter-from-margaret-sanger-to-dr-cj-gamble-annotated.
3. John J. Conley, S. J., "Margaret Sanger was a eugenicist. Why are we still celebrating her?" *America: The Jesuit Review*, November 27, 2017, https://www.americamagazine.org/politics-society/2017/11/27/margaret-sanger-was-eugenicist-why-are-we-still-celebrating-her.
4. "Hillary Clinton Honors Margaret Sanger at the 2009 Planned Parenthood Honors Gala," YouTube video, 1:20, November 15, 2009, https://www.youtube.com/watch?v=r4o4WizW2mQ.
5. Jennifer Latson, "What Margaret Sanger Really Said About Eugenics and Race," *Time*, October 14, 2016, https://time.com/4081760/margaret-sanger-history-eugenics/.
6. Gloria Steinem, "Margaret Sanger: Her crusade to legalize birth control spurred the movement for women's liberation," *Time*, April 13, 1998, https://content.time.com/time/subscriber/article/0,33009,988152-1,00.html.
7. Ema O'Connor, "Employees Are Calling Out Major Reproductive Rights Organizations For Racism And Hypocrisy," Buzzfeed News, August 21, 2020, https://www.buzzfeednews.com/article/emaoconnor/employees-calling-out-reproductive-rights-groups.
8. Jake Silverstein, "Editor's Note," *The New York Times Magazine*, August 18, 2019, https://pulitzercenter.org/sites/default/files/full_issue_of_the_1619_project.pdf.
9. Later came the book *The 1619 Project: A New Origin Story* by Nikole Hannah-Jones and a television series on Hulu.
10. Victoria Bynum, James M. McPherson, James Oakes, Sean Wilentz, Gordon S. Wood, letter to the editor, *The New York Times Magazine*, December 20, 2019.
11. Alexis McGill Johnson: "I'm the Head of Planned Parenthood. We're Done Making Excuses for Our Founder," *The New York Times*, April 17, 2021, https://www.nytimes.com/2021/04/17/opinion/planned-parenthood-margaret-sanger.html.
12. In truth, this was really the second such alliance. In 2017, after Donald Trump was sworn in as president of the United States, Cecile Richards left her post as presi-

dent of the Planned Parenthood Federation of America to join Ai-jenn Poo and Alicia Garza, one of the co-founders of Black Lives Matter, Inc., to establish Supermajority, "an organization focused on making women the most feared and revered voting bloc in the country."
13. *Political Correctness: A Deceptive and Dangerous Worldview*, edited by William Lind and Richard Hawkins, Nehemiah Institute, Winter Garden, FL, 2004, 63-64.
14. Lawrence Lader and Milton Meltzer, *Margaret Sanger: Pioneer of Birth Control* (New York: Thomas Crowell Co., 1969), 163.
15. G. K. Chesterton, *Illustrated London News*, September 26, 1908. As Quoted in *G.K. Chesterton: Collected Works, Volume XXVIII: The Illustrated London News 1908-1910* (San Francisco: Ignatius Press, 1987), 186.

2. THE UNHOLY TRINITY OF DEPRAVITY AND DEATH

1. George Grant, *Grand Illusions: The Legacy of Planned Parenthood*, second ed. (Franklin, Tennessee: Adroit Press, 1992), 96.
2. Leon F. Whitney's unpublished autobiography, written in 1971, Whitney Papers, APS, 204–205, cited in Mike Richmond, "Margaret Sanger, Sterilization, and the Swastika," The Ethical Spectacle, accessed November 9, 2023, https://www.spectacle.org/997/richmond.html.
3. Stefan Kuhl, *The Nazi Connection: Eugenics, American Racism, and German National Socialism* (Oxford: Oxford University Press, 1994), 85.
4. This German word *Übermensch* literally means "overman." The term *Übermensch* was frequently used by Hitler and the Nazi party to describe their concept of the biologically superior Aryan. This was contrasted with the German word for the biologically inferior and unfit: *Untermensch*. Translated as "underman" or "subhuman." Both the American Eugenics Society and the Third Reich believed the "underman" must be suppressed or eliminated in order to preserve the integrity, flourishing, and future of the "overman." American eugenicists spoke of this same concept with the words "fit" and "unfit."
5. Leon Whitney, *The Case for Sterilization* (New York: Frederick A. Stokes; 1934), 136, Accessed, https://www.docdroid.net/TpAtrRg/the-case-for-sterilization-by-leon-f-whitney-1934-pdf.
6. Edwin Black, *War Against the Weak: Eugenics and America's Campaign To Create a Master Race* (Washington DC: Dialog Press, 2012), 274-275.
7. Paul A. Offit, "The Loathsome American Book That Inspired Hitler," *The Daily Beast*, August 26, 2017, https://www.thedailybeast.com/the-loathsome-american-book-that-inspired-hitler.
8. Madison Grant, *The Passing of the Great Race* (New York: Charles Scribner's Sons, 1936), 49. Accessed March 27, 2024 at, https://archive.org/details/the-passing-of-the-great-race/page/48/mode/2up.
9. Jonathan Peter Spiro, *Defending the Master Race: Conservation, Eugenics, and the Legacy of Madison Grant* (Lebanon: University of Vermont Press, 2009), 48.
10. Edwin Black, *War Against the Weak*, 138-139.
11. Margaret Sanger, "Birth Control and Racial Betterment," *Birth Control Review*, February 1919, PDF, 12, https://lifedynamics.com/wp-content/uploads/2023/01/1919-02-February.pdf.

NOTES

12. Margaret Sanger, *The Pivot of Civilization* (New York: Brentano's, 1922) 82, 101, https://archive.org/details/pivotofcivilizat00sanguoft/page/n9/mode/2up.
13. Margaret Sanger, *The Woman Rebel*, vol. 1, no. 1, March, 1914, https://libcom.org/article/woman-rebel.
14. Thomas Malthus, "An Essay on the Principle of Population," *Essays on the Principle of Population*, Sixth Edition (1826), Book IV, Chapter V, EconLib, February 5, 2018, https://www.econlib.org/library/Malthus/malPlong.html?chapter_num=47#book-reader.
15. George Grant, *Grand Illusions*, 56.
16. Madeline Gray, *Margaret Sanger: A Biography of the Champion of Birth Control*, (NY: Richard Marek Publisher, 1979), 87-93, 97-100.
17. Germaine Greer, *Sex and Destiny: The Politics of Human Fertility* (New York: Harper and Row, 1984), 308.
18. Ibid., 307.
19. Charles Darwin, *The Descent of Man*, 2 vols. [1871] (Princeton, NJ: Princeton University Press, 1981), 1:201.
20. Grant, *Grand Illusions*, 57–58.
21. The phrase "ideas have consequences" was coined by Richard Weaver and is the title of his famous 1948 book. The phrase "bad ideas have victims" I first heard used by John Stonestreet, President of the Colson Center for Worldview.
22. Edwin Black, *War Against the Weak*, 133.
23. Günther at a meeting of the "'Kampfbundes fur deutsche Kultur'" on February 21, 1934. "Der Vererbungs- und Rassegedanke innerhalb der Einwanderungsgesetzgebung," *Volkischer Beobachter* (February 23, 1934). See Stefan Kuhl, *The Nazi Connection: Eugenics, American Racism, and German National Socialism* (Oxford: Oxford University Press, 1994), 38–39.
24. William L. Shirer, *Berlin Diary: The Journal of a Foreign Correspondent* (New York: Alfred Knopf, 1941), 257.
25. Williams, Cameron, "A Study of the United States Influence on German Eugenics" (2020). Electronic Theses and Dissertations, Paper 3781, page 12, https://dc.etsu.edu/etd/3781.
26. Lothrop Stoddard, *Into the Darkness: An Uncensored Report from Inside the Third Reich At War* (Los Angeles: Indo-European Publishing, 2011), 161.
27. Ibid., 152.
28. Lothrop Stoddard, *The Rising Tide of Color against White World Supremacy* (New York: Charles Scribner's Sons, 1926), 259-260, as quoted in Edwin Black, *War Against the Weak*, 91.
29. George Grant, *Killer Angel: A Biography of Planned Parenthood's Founder Margaret Sanger* (Nashville, TN: Cumberland House, 2001), 84.
30. Ernst Rüdin, "Eugenic Sterilization: An Urgent Need," *Birth Control Review*, 17, 103, https://lifedynamics.com/wp-content/uploads/2023/01/1933-04-April.pdf.
31. Grant, *Grand Illusions*, 96.
32. Citizens Commission on Human Rights editors, "Chronology of Psychology's Role in Creating the Holocaust," Citizens Commission on Human Rights, accessed March 6, 2024, https://www.cchr.org/documentaries/age-of-fear/creating-the-holocaust.html.
33. Robert Jay Lifton, *The Nazi Doctors: Medical Killing and the Psychology of Genocide* (NewYork: Basic Books, 1986), 27.

NOTES

34. M. M. Weber, "Ernst Rüdin, 1874–1952: A German psychiatrist and geneticist," *American Journal of Medicine*, Genet., 67: 323–331, https://doi.org/10.1002/(SICI)1096-8628(19960726)67:4<323::AID-AJMG2>3.0.CO;2-N.
35. Gerald L. Posner and John Ware, *Mengele: The Complete Story* (New York: McGraw-Hill Book Company, 1986), 9.
36. Grant, *Grand Illusions*, 61.
37. Edwin Black, "Hitler's debt to America," *The Guardian*, February 5, 2004, https://www.theguardian.com/uk/2004/feb/06/race.usa.

3. THE THEOLOGICAL ROOTS OF EVIL

1. History.com Editors, "November 4, 2008: Proposition 8 is passed in California, banning same-sex marriage," This Day in History, History, updated June 30, 2022, https://www.history.com/this-day-in-history/prop-8-passed-california-gay-marriage.
2. SB 729.
3. AB 665.
4. AB 957.
5. AB 598.
6. AB 315.
7. "FULL SPEECH: Tucker Carlson's Last Address Before Leaving Fox News at #Heritage50," YouTube video, 36:44, April 25, 2023, https://www.youtube.com/watch?v=N32UPXGChgo.
8. David Goldstein, *Suicide Bent: Sangerizing America* (St. Paul: Radio Replies Press, 1945), 103.
9. Hilaire Belloc, *The Cruise of the Nona* (London: Constable and Co, 1925), accessed March 31, 2024, https://archive.org/stream/in.ernet.dli.2015.227789/2015.227789.The-Cruise_djvu.txt.
10. Michael S. Heiser, *The Unseen Realm: Recovering the Supernatural Worldview of the Bible* (Bellingham, WA: Lexham Press, 2015), 114.
11. Herbert Marcuse, *Eros and Civilization* (Boston: Beacon Press, 1966), 198.
12. Margaret Sanger, *The Pivot of Civilization* (1922), Project Gutenberg, updated February 8, 2013, https://www.gutenberg.org/cache/epub/1689/pg1689-images.html.
13. Jonathan Cahn, *The Return of the Gods* (Lake Mary, FL: Frontline, 2022), 88.
14. "FULL SPEECH: Tucker Carlson's Last Address Before Leaving Fox News at #Heritage50."
15. Cahn, *The Return of the Gods*, 88.
16. Herbert Schlossberg, *Idols for Destruction* (Wheaton: Crossway, 1990), 295.
17. Rainer Zitelmann, "Is Capitalism to Blame for Hunger and Poverty?" Adam Smith Institute, June 24, 2021, https://www.adamsmith.org/blog/is-capitalism-to-blame-for-hunger-and-poverty.
18. *Gnosis* is the Greek word for "knowledge"; hence, "Gnosticism."
19. C. S. Lewis, *The Case for Christianity* (New York: Simon & Schuster, 1996), 32.
20. Nancy Pearcey, *Love Thy Body* (Grand Rapids: Baker Books, 2018), 36.
21. Nancy Pearcey, *Love Thy Body* (Grand Rapids: Baker Books, 2018), 50.

22. Ibid.
23. Peter Singer, *Practical Ethics*, 2nd ed. (Cambridge: Cambridge University Press, 1993), 85–86.
24. Nancy Pearcey, *Love Thy Body*, 254–255.
25. These comments were made by my friend Pastor Jack Hibbs at a conference called Sacred: Made in the Image of God, held March 7, 2021, at Heritage Church in Escalon, California. See "Sacred: Made in the Image of God with Jack Hibbs and Seth Gruber," YouTube video, 1:55:22, March 23, 2021, https://www.youtube.com/watch?v=fr5-X0GxZ3A.
26. Cory Booker, WSUF 89.9 FM, October 15, 2019, 10:00 p.m.–11:00 p.m. EDT, https://archive.org/details/WSUF_89_9_FM_20191016_020000?start=1275.
27. *Merriam-Webster*, s.v. "sacrosanct (*adj.*)," accessed October 2, 2023, https://www.merriam-webster.com/dictionary/sacrosanct.
28. Eric Metaxas, *Letter to the American Church* (Washington, D.C.: Salem Books, 2022), 43.
29. Ibid., 44–45.
30. *Testament to Freedom: The Essential Writings of Dietrich Bonhoeffer*, ed. Kelly & Nelson (Harper San Francisco, 1990), 139.

4. 1916 AND THE RACE TO DESTROY THE "UNFIT"

1. Grant, *The Grand Illusion*, 27.
2. "Intelligent or Unintelligent Birth Control," *The Birth Control Review*, May 1919, 12, PDF, https://lifedynamics.com/wp-content/uploads/2023/01/1919-05-May.pdf.
3. "The Eugenic Value of Birth Control Propaganda," *The Birth Control Review*, October 1921, 5, PDF, https://lifedynamics.com/wp-content/uploads/2023/01/1921-10-October.pdf.
4. Margaret Sanger, *The Pivot of Civilization* (New York: Brentano's, 1922) 101, 102, 265, 264, 90, https://archive.org/details/pivotofcivilizat00sanguoft/page/n9/mode/2up.
5. Jonathan Peter Spiro, *Defending the Master Race*, 194.
6. Margaret Sanger, "Birth Control and Racial Betterment," *Birth Control Review*, February 1919, PDF, 12, https://lifedynamics.com/wp-content/uploads/2023/01/1919-02-February.pdf.
7. Matthew 7:27 [emphasis added].
8. Matthew 7:25.
9. "Fact Sheet," Planned Parenthood Federation of America, Inc., October 2004, PDF, https://www.plannedparenthood.org/files/8013/9611/6937/Opposition_Claims_About_Margaret_Sanger.pdf.
10. Margaret Sanger, "APOSTLE OF BIRTH CONTROL SEES CAUSE GAINING HERE; Hearing in Albany on Bill to Legalize Practice a Milestone in Long Fight of Margaret Sanger—Even China Awakening to Need of Selective Methods, She Says," *The New York Times*, April 8, 1923, https://www.nytimes.com/1923/04/08/archives/apostle-of-birth-control-sees-cause-gaining-here-hearing-in-albany.html.

NOTES

11. 274 U.S. 200 (*Buck v. Bell*) Archived 2011-10-09 at the Wayback Machine, Justia.com U.S. Supreme Court Center Archived 2021-05-06 at the Wayback Machine.
12. Editors at *Fresh Air*, "The Supreme Court Ruling That Led To 70,000 Forced Sterilizations," *Fresh Air*, National Public Radio, March 7, 2016, https://www.npr.org/sections/health-shots/2016/03/07/469478098/the-supreme-court-ruling-that-led-to-70-000-forced-sterilizations.
13. Planned Parenthood. "Our History" PlannedParenthood.org, https://www.plannedparenthood.org/about-us/who-we-are/our-history. Accessed March 28, 2024.
14. Edwin Black, "Eugenics and the Nazis—the California connection," *SFGATE*, Nov. 9, 2003, https://www.sfgate.com/opinion/article/Eugenics-and-the-Nazis-the-California-2549771.php.
15. Ibid.
16. Margaret Sanger, "A Plan for Peace," *Birth Control Review*, April 1932, PDF, 107–108, https://lifedynamics.com/wp-content/uploads/2023/01/1932-04-April.pdf.
17. Mark Joyella, "Hillary Clinton Suggests 'Formal Deprogramming' For 'MAGA Extremists' Who Still Support Trump," *Forbes*, October 6, 2023, https://www.forbes.com/sites/markjoyella/2023/10/06/hillary-clinton-suggests-formal-deprogramming-for-maga-extremists-who-still-support-trump/?sh=209750ab73b8.
18. Margaret Sanger, ed., *International Aspects of Birth Control: The International Neo-Malthusian and Birth Control Conference*. New York: American Birth Control League, 1925, p.v., quoted in Grant, *Killer Angel*, 91-92.
19. See Jared Eckert and Emma Sofia Mull, "Planned Parenthood Profits Big From Getting Kids Hooked On Transgender Hormones Through The School-To-Clinic Pipeline," The Federalist, May 10, 2022, https://thefederalist.com/2022/05/10/planned-parenthood-profits-big-from-getting-kids-hooked-on-transgender-hormones-through-the-school-to-clinic-pipeline/.
20. U.S. Senate Committee On Health, Education, Labor & Pensions, "Ranking Member Cassidy Calls out Planned Parenthood's Opaque Reporting and Questions its use of Taxpayer Dollars to Fund Gender Transition Services," Help.Senate.Gov, November 28, 2023, Accessed April 1, 2024, https://www.help.senate.gov/ranking/newsroom/press/ranking-member-cassidy-calls-out-planned-parenthoods-opaque-reporting-and-questions-its-use-of-taxpayer-dollars-to-fund-gender-transition-services
21. See "Survey of 490 neonatologists," *Journal of Medical Ethics*, March 17, 2016.
22. Rachel K. Jones and Amy Friedrich-Karnik, "Medication Abortion Accounted for 63% of All US Abortions in 2023—An Increase from 53% in 2020," Guttmacher Institute, March 19, 2024, https://www.guttmacher.org/2024/03/medication-abortion-accounted-63-all-us-abortions-2023-increase-53-2020.
23. "Hoescht AG," ChemEurope, accessed April 22, 2024, https://www.chemeurope.com/en/encyclopedia/Hoechst_AG.html.
24. "IG Farben," ChemEurope, accessed April 22, 2024, https://www.chemeurope.com/en/encyclopedia/IG_Farben.html.
25. "Hoescht AG," ChemEurope, accessed April 22, 2024, https://www.chemeurope.com/en/encyclopedia/Hoechst_AG.html.
26. Luther Turmelle, "Hoescht AG to buy out Rousell Uclaf," *The Courier-News*, December 12, 1996, 20, https://mycentraljersey.newspapers.com/image/222599691/?clipping_id=22221726&fcfToken=eyJhbGciOiJIUzI1NiIsInR5c

NOTES

163

CI6IkpXVCJ9.eyJmcmVlLXZpZXctaWQiOjIyMjU5OTY5MSwiaWF0IjoxNzEz
ODQ5MDk5LCJleHAiOjE3MTM5MzU0OTl9.
zBuxBF8gJCljTngxzPWJ00bvHDE1cFhK8zcNNFjNrJU.

27. Margaret Sanger, *The Pivot of Civilization* (New York: Brentano's, 1922), 101, as quoted in Grant, *Killer Angel*, 79-80.
28. Grant, *Killer Angel: A Biography of Planned Parenthood's Founder Margaret Sanger*, 97.
29. See "Proceedings of the World population conference : held at the Salle centrale, Geneva, August 29th to September 3rd, 1927 / edited by Mrs. Margaret Sanger.," https://wellcomecollection.org/works/p9g7uhez.
30. "Topic: German/Nazi Eugenics," Eugenics Archive, accessed March 25, 2024, http://www.eugenicsarchive.org/eugenics/topics_fs.pl?theme=41&search=& matches=.
31. Edwin Black, "In Germany's extermination program for black Africans, a template for the Holocaust," *The Times of Israel*, May 5, 2016, https://www.timesofisrael.com/in-germanys-extermination-program-for-black-africans-a-template-for-the-holocaust/.
32. Edwin Black, *War Against the Weak*, 317.
33. Citizens Commission on Human Rights editors, "Chronology of Psychology's Role in Creating the Holocaust," Citizens Commission on Human Rights, accessed March 25, 2024, https://www.cchr.org/documentaries/age-of-fear/creating-the-holocaust.html.
34. Ibid.
35. Ibid.
36. Edwin Black, *War Against the Weak*, 347.
37. Ibid.
38. Ibid., 354.
39. "Topic: Twin Studies," Eugenics Archive, accessed March 7, 2024, http://www.eugenicsarchive.org/eugenics/topics_fs.pl?theme=30&search=&matches=.
40. Edwin Black, *War Against the Weak*, 348.
41. Edwin Black, "In Germany's extermination program for black Africans, a template for the Holocaust," *The Times of Israel*, May 5, 2016, https://www.timesofisrael.com/in-germanys-extermination-program-for-black-africans-a-template-for-the-holocaust/.
42. Daniel Keane, "Nazi scientist Otmar von Verschuer's correspondence with British biologist illuminates corruption of medicine," ABC (Australia) Radio News, August 30, 2022, https://www.abc.net.au/news/2022-08-31/verschuer-fisher-letters-on-tobacco-and-nazi-medicine/101376720.
43. Miklos Nyiszli, *Auschwitz: A Doctor's Eyewitness Account* (New York: Frederick Fell, 1960), quoted in Stefan Kuhl, *The Nazi Connection: Eugenics, American Racism, and German National Socialism* (Oxford: Oxford University Press, 1994), 103.
44. Edwin Black, *War Against the Weak*, 363.
45. Ibid., 359.
46. Congressional Hearing - Planned Parenthood Abortion Trainer: "An Eyeball Just Fell Down Into My Lap," YouTube video, 0:32, March 22, 2024, https://www.youtube.com/watch?v=8QPSNujRmKk&t=51s.

47. Linda Gordon, *Woman's Body, Woman's Right: Birth Control In America* (New York: Penguin Group, 1990), 328.
48. Margaret Sanger, "Letter from Margaret Sanger to Dr. C. J. Gamble," Genius, Accessed October 29, 2023, https://genius.com/Margaret-sanger-letter-from-margaret-sanger-to-dr-cj-gamble-annotated.
49. As quoted in Grant, *Grand Illusions*, 97.
50. Micaiah Bilger, "Planned Parenthood Puts 86% of Its Abortion Facilities in Minority Neighborhoods," LifeNews.com, September 23, 2020, https://www.lifenews.com/2020/09/23/planned-parenthood-puts-86-of-its-abortion-facilities-in-minority-neighborhoods/.
51. Susan Willke Enouen, "Research Shows Planned Parenthood Expands Targeting Minorities as it Spurns Racist Founder," Townhall, September 23, 2020, https://townhall.com/columnists/susanwillkeenouen/2020/09/23/research-shows-planned-parenthood-expands-targeting-minorities-as-it-spurns-racist-founder-n2576680.
52. Ryan Bomberger, "Planned Parenthood Kills More Black Lives in 2 Weeks Than the KKK Killed in a Century," ChristianPost.com, July 17, 2018, https://www.christianpost.com/voices/planned-parenthood-kills-more-black-lives-in-2-weeks-than-the-kkk-killed-in-a-century.html.
53. Margaret Sanger to Clarence Gamble, Oct. 19, 1939 as quoted in Gordon, *Woman's Body, Woman's Right*, 328.
54. Billy Hallowell, "Why Lecrae Was Almost 'Done' With Christianity: Rapper Tackles Race, Raphael Warnock Controversy, and a 'Very, Very Dark' Time in His Life," FaithWire, April 27, 2022, https://www.faithwire.com/2022/04/27/why-lecrae-was-almost-done-with-christianity-rapper-tackles-race-raphael-warnock-controversy-and-a-very-very-dark-time-in-his-life/.
55. J. D. Hall, "Lecrae, Carl Lentz, Fawn Over Pro-Abortion Democrat, Stacey Abrams," Pulpit & Pen, November 20, 2018, https://pulpitandpen.org/2018/11/20/lecrae-carl-lentz-fawn-over-pro-abortion-democrat-stacey-abrams/.
56. Jack Birle, "Planned Parenthood changes website after Stacey Abrams's heartbeat comments," Restoring America, *Washington Examiner*, September 23, 2022, https://www.washingtonexaminer.com/restoring-america/community-family/planned-parenthood-changes-website-abrams-heartbeat-comments.
57. Ibid.
58. Jesse T. Jackson, "Sean Feucht, Charlie Kirk Call Out T.D. Jakes for Welcoming Pro-Choice Politician Beto O'Rourke at The Potter's House," ChurchLeaders, October 25, 2022, https://churchleaders.com/news/437142-sean-feucht-charlie-kirk-call-out-t-d-jakes-for-welcoming-pro-choice-politician-beto-orourke-at-the-potters-house.html.
59. Houston Keene, "Beto O'Rourke won't say whether he supports any limit on abortion," Fox News, September 1, 2022, https://www.foxnews.com/politics/beto-orourke-wont-say-supports-limit-abortion.
60. "TAKEDOWN: Emmanuel Acho's "Uncomfortable" *Roe v. Wade* Conversation | Guest: John Amanchukwu," YouTube video, 8:45, July 19, 2022, https://www.youtube.com/watch?v=udnxrtcrjf8&list=PLlXQ-jkBULm8p3XF4MpAZ9DS6YddhQfwB&index=83.

5. 1916 AND THE SEXUAL REVOLUTION

1. Madeline Gray, *Margaret Sanger: A Biography of the Champion of Birth Control* (New York: Richard Marek Publishers, 1979), 58–59.
2. Margaret Sanger, *The Woman Rebel*, volume 1, issue 1, March 1914. Reprinted in Margaret Sanger, *Woman and the New Race* (New York: Brentano's Publishers, 1922).
3. Grant, *Grand Illusions*, 117–118.
4. Washington Star News, May 3, 1973. Accessed here: https://ce5835e7-790b-44f3-ba83-3d60bf9f6735.filesusr.com/ugd/4cf5ff_8a86419f f2904cbe99d1b8ac6ad39442.pdf?index=true.
5. Pamela J. Maraldo, "Contraceptive Use: Coping With Psychosocial Barriers," *Family Planning World*, 3–4/93, 5, https://www.ewtn.com/catholicism/library/who-was-margaret-sanger-12137.
6. Stop CSE Editors, "The History & Agenda Behind CSE," Family Watch, accessed November 2, 2023, https://www.comprehensivesexualityeducation.org/history-of-cse/.
7. Claire Chambers, *The SIECUS Circle: A Humanist Revolution* (Belmont, MA: Western Islands, 1977), 12.
8. George Grant, *Grand Illusions*, 197.
9. Claire Chambers, *The SIECUS Circle*, 12.
10. Ibid., 12.
11. Ibid., 12.
12. Ibid., 6.
13. William F. Jasper, "Normalizing Child Rape: The Decades-long Kinsey-Rockefeller-Playboy Push That Produced Our Current Pedophile Crisis," *The New American*, July 20, 2023, https://thenewamerican.com/us/culture/normalizing-child-rape-the-decades-long-kinsey-rockefeller-playboy-push-that-produced-our-current-pedophile-crisis/.
14. Miriam Grossman, "A Brief History of Sex Ed: How We Reached Today's Madness," *Public Discourse: The Journal of the Witherspoon Institute*, July 16, 2013, https://www.thepublicdiscourse.com/2013/07/10408/.
15. Ibid.
16. Jonathan Gathorne-Hardy, *Sex the Measure of All Things: A Life of Alfred C. Kinsey* (Bloomington, IN: Indiana University Press, 1998), 31.
17. Claire Chambers, *The SIECUS Circle: A Humanist Revolution* (Belmont, MA: Western Islands, 1977), 51.
18. Lester A. Kirkendall, *Sex Education*, SIECUS Study Guide No. 1, Fourth Printing, January 1969 (New York: SIECUS Publications Office), 15.
19. Judith A. Reisman and Edward W. Eichel, *Kinsey, Sex and Fraud: The Indoctrination of a People*, (Lafayette, IN: Lochinvar Inc., 1990), 128.
20. Ibid., 129.
21. Mary S. Calderone, "Fetal Erection and Its Message to Us," *SIECUS Report*, May–July 1983, 9-10, quoted in Reisman and Eichel, *Kinsey, Sex and Fraud*, 129.
22. Mary S. Calderone, "Childhood, the First Season: Nurturing Sexual Awakening—A Panel Discussion of Masturbation, Sex Play, Sexual Abuse, Nudity and Body

Images Issues," SSSS Eastern Region Conference, *The Seasons of Sexology: Cycles of Time*, April 20, 1985, quoted in Reisman and Eichel, *Kinsey, Sex and Fraud*, 129.
23. Dina Spector, "Why Kinsey's Research Remains Even More Controversial Than The 'Masters Of Sex'," *Business Insider*, October 18, 2013, https://www.businessinsider.com/why-alfred-kinsey-was-controversial-2013-10?op=1.
24. Ibid.
25. James H. Jones, *Alfred C. Kinsey: A Public/Private Life* (New York: W. W. Norton, 1997), 511.
26. Reisman and Eichel, *Kinsey, Sex and Fraud*, 6.
27. Mary Faulds, "10 men who destroyed American culture," *American Family Association Journal*, accessed March 22, 2024, https://afajournal.org/past-issues/2010/march/10-men-who-destroyed-american-culture/.
28. Barbara Kay, "Barbara Kay: To understand Bill Cosby, start with Alfred C. Kinsey," *National Post*, July 29, 2015, https://nationalpost.com/opinion/barbara-kay-to-understand-bill-cosby-start-with-alfred-c-kinsey.
29. Reisman and Eichel, *Kinsey, Sex and Fraud*, 44.
30. Judith A. Reisman, *Kinsey: Crimes & Consequences*, Fourth Edition (Arlington, Virginia: Institute for Media Education, 2012), 165.
31. Ibid., 166.
32. Ibid., 165.
33. Ibid.
34. Ibid., 166–167.
35. Ibid., 166.
36. Ibid.
37. Wardell B. Pomeroy, "A New Look at Incest," *Variations* (magazine), January 1977, pages 86 to 88, as quoted in Reisman and Eichel, *Kinsey, Sex and Fraud*, 70.
38. Reisman, *Kinsey: Crimes & Consequences*, 177.
39. See siecus.org.
40. Grant, *Grand Illusions*, 110.
41. James D. Bratt, ed., *Abraham Kuyper: A Centennial Reader* (Grand Rapids: William B. Eerdmans, 1998), 473.
42. Leonard Gross, "Sex Education Comes of Age," *Look Magazine*, March 8, 1966, as quoted in Grant, *Grand Illusions*, 11.
43. Grant, *Grand Illusions*, 110–111.
44. Reisman, *Kinsey: Crimes & Consequences*, First Edition (Arlington, Virginia, Institute for Media Education, 1998), 180.
45. Sanger coined the term *birth control*. Notice it's not the same as *contraceptive*, which carries the technical meaning of "a device or preparation that is designed to prevent conception." (See *Merriam-Webster*, s.v. "contraceptive (*n.*)," accessed November 4, 2023, https://www.merriam-webster.com/dictionary/contraceptive) Birth control is not designed to prevent the creation of a child; it's designed to stop the child from being born, and so includes every abortifacient imaginable. For Sanger, it was never really about "planned parenthood"; it was about the death of the unborn by any means necessary.
46. Margaret Sanger, *My Fight for Birth Control* (New York NY: Farrar & Rinehart, 1931), 12-13.
47. Ibid., 13.

48. "Fact Sheet," Planned Parenthood Federation of America, Inc., October 2004, PDF, https://www.plannedparenthood.org/files/8013/9611/6937/Opposition_Claims_About_Margaret_Sanger.pdf.
49. Margaret Sanger, *Woman and the New Race* (New York: Truth Publishing Co., 1920), 63.
50. Wake Forest University Students, *Gender & Sexuality: A Transnational Anthology from 1690 to 1990*, online (Wake Forest, North Carolina: Wake Forest University Press, 2019), https://librarypartnerspress.pressbooks.pub/gendersexuality1e/.
51. Margaret Sanger, *Family Limitation* (New York: Margaret Sanger, 1916), accessed March 31, 2024, at https://archive.lib.msu.edu/DMC/AmRad/familylimitations.pdf.
52. Sanger, *Woman and the New Race*, 119–120.
53. This line became the chant of the abortion movement following the overturning of *Roe v. Wade*. Two pro-abortion activist and terrorist groups, Jane's Revenge and Ruth Sent Us, began interrupting church services following the overturning of *Roe*, dressed in *The Handmaid's Tale* outfits, chanting, "Without this basic right women can't be free! Abortions on demand and without apology!"
54. Some translations describe Gideon using two bulls for the task. The Hebrew is ambiguous and it's possible he used a single bull or two bulls. Either way, since Baal was often depicted as a bull, it was poetic. Gideon used a bull to tear down an altar to the bull.
55. Anna K. Miller and Scott Yenor, *The Sex Ed Industrial Complex: How Conservative School Districts Come to Peddle Radical Sex Education to Children*, Claremont Press, PDF, accessed January 3, 2024, https://dc.claremont.org/wp-content/uploads/2023/02/The-Sex-Ed-Industrial-Complex.pdf.
56. Planned Parenthood. "What is Sex Education?" PlannedParenthood.org, https://www.plannedparenthood.org/learn/for-educators/what-sex-education. Accessed March 26, 2024.
57. Jared Miller, "Planned Parenthood Memo from 1969 Exposes the Left's Long-Term Blueprint for Population Control," *The Western Journal*, October 23, 2022, https://www.westernjournal.com/planned-parenthood-memo-1969-exposes-lefts-long-term-blueprint-population-control/.

6. WOKE AS WOLVES

1. Jean-Jacques Rousseau, *Social Contract and Discourses*, trans. G. D. H. Cole (New York: E. P. Dutton, 1950), 136.
2. Benjamin Wallace-Wells, "David French, Sohrab Ahmari, and the Battle for the Future of Conservatism," *The New Yorker*, September 12, 2019, https://www.newyorker.com/news/the-political-scene/david-french-sohrab-ahmari-and-the-battle-for-the-future-of-conservatism.
3. Tim Keller, "Religion-Less Spirituality," *Christianity Today*, Fall 1999, https://www.christianitytoday.com/pastors/1999/fall/9l4025.html.
4. Ibid.
5. Michael Foust, "Tim Keller Explains Why He's a Registered Democrat: It's 'Smart Voting' and Strategic," Christian Headlines, November 5, 2020, https://www.

christianheadlines.com/contributors/michael-foust/tim-keller-explains-why-hes-a-registered-democrat-its-smart-voting-and-strategic.html.

6. Timothy Keller (@timkellernyc), "Christians and the freedom of conscience in politics," Twitter, September 16, 2020, https://twitter.com/timkellernyc/status/1306401474222620672.
7. Timothy Keller, "How Do Christians Fit into the Two-Party System? They Don't" *The New York Times*, September 29, 2018, https://www.nytimes.com/2018/09/29/opinion/sunday/christians-politics-belief.html.
8. Ibid.
9. See *God + Country: The Rise of Christian Nationalism*, directed by Dan Partland, Oscilloscope Laboratories, 2024.
10. Madeline Osburn, "University Of Pittsburgh Uses Taxpayer-Funded Aborted Babies For Medical Research," The Federalist, May 7, 2021, https://thefederalist.com/2021/05/07/university-of-pittsburgh-uses-taxpayer-funded-aborted-babies-for-medical-research/.
11. "BREAKING: University of Pittsburgh ADMITS Hearts Beating While Harvesting Aborted Infants' Kidneys," Center for Medical Progress, August 4, 2021, https://www.centerformedicalprogress.org/2021/08/breaking-university-of-pittsburgh-admits-hearts-beating-while-harvesting-aborted-infants-kidneys/.
12. Judicial Watch, "Judicial Watch: New HHS Documents Reveal Millions in Federal Funding for University of Pittsburgh Human Fetal Organ Harvesting Project Including Viable and Full-Term Babies," Judicial Watch, August 3, 2021, https://www.judicialwatch.org/hhs-documents-organ-harvesting/.
13. John G. West, "NIH Director Francis Collins Isn't A National Treasure, He's A National Disgrace," Discovery Institute, October 8, 2021, https://www.discovery.org/a/nih-director-francis-collins-isnt-a-national-treasure-hes-a-national-disgrace/.
14. "The COVID-19 Vaccines: A Conversation with Dr. Francis Collins," YouTube video, 31:39, December 3, 2020, https://www.youtube.com/watch?v=Er7XjryDHkg.
15. "Transcript: All In with Chris Hayes, 9/9/21," MSNBC, September 9, 2021, https://www.msnbc.com/transcripts/transcript-all-chris-hayes-9-9-21-n1278904.
16. "Updated Assessment on COVID-19 Origins," Office of the Director of National Intelligence, National Intelligence Council, accessed January 18, 2024, https://www.dni.gov/files/ODNI/documents/assessments/Declassified-Assessment-on-COVID-19-Origins.pdf.
17. Madeline Coggins, "GOP senator releases 'bombshell' COVID-19 origins report," Fox Business, April 18, 2023, https://www.foxbusiness.com/politics/gop-sentor-releases-bombshell-covid-origins-report.
18. Meredith Wadman and *Nature Magazine*, "The Truth about Fetal Tissue Research," *Scientific American*, December 9, 2015, https://www.scientificamerican.com/article/the-truth-about-fetal-tissue-research/#:~:text=This%20model%20is%20made%20by,from%20the%20same%20fetal%20liver.
19. John Zmirak, "I Oppose 'Public Health,' and You Should Too," The Stream, October 1, 2021, https://stream.org/i-oppose-public-health-and-you-should-too/.
20. Suzan Sammons, "Covid Jabs Revealed Hidden Pro-life Heroes," *Crisis Magazine*, June 30, 2022, https://crisismagazine.com/opinion/covid-jabs-revealed-hidden-pro-life-heroes.

21. Julie Collorafi, "To Save Ourselves From COVID, We're Sacrificing Children, Part 2: "Humanized" Mice and the Birth of COVID," The Stream, November 21, 2021, https://stream.org/to-save-ourselves-from-covid-were-sacrificing-children-part-2-humanized-mice/.
22. Declan Butler, "Engineered bat virus stirs debate over risky research," Nature, November 12, 2015, https://www.nature.com/articles/nature.2015.18787#Bib1.
23. Ren-Di Jiang, Mei-Qin Liu, Ying Chen, Chao Shan, Yi-Wu Zhou, Xu-Rui Shen, Qian Li, Lei Zhang, Yan Zhu, Hao-Rui Si, Qi Wang, Juan Min, Xi Wang, Wei Zhang, Bei Li, Hua-Jun Zhang, Ralph S. Baric, Peng Zhou, Xing-Lou Yang, and Zheng-Li Shi, "Pathogenesis of SARS-CoV-2 in Transgenic Mice Expressing Human Angiotensin-Converting Enzyme 2," National Library of Medicine, May 21, 2020, https://www.ncbi.nlm.nih.gov/pmc/articles/PMC7241398/.
24. Julie Collorafi, "To Save Ourselves From COVID, We're Sacrificing Children, Part 2: "Humanized" Mice and the Birth of COVID."
25. Ibid.
26. Julie Collorafi, "To Save Ourselves From COVID, We're Sacrificing Children, Part 3: More Baby Parts Are Needed All the Time," The Stream, November 22, 2021, https://stream.org/to-save-ourselves-from-covid-were-sacrificing-children-part-3-more-baby-parts-are-needed-all-the-time/.
27. Angela Wahl, Chandrav De, Maria Abad Fernandez, Erik M. Lenarcic, Yinyan Xu, Adam S. Cockrell, Rachel A. Cleary, Claire E. Johnson, Nathaniel J. Schramm, Laura M. Rank, Isabel G. Newsome, Heather A. Vincent, Wes Sanders, Christian R. Aguilera-Sandoval, Allison Boone, William H. Hildebrand, Paul A. Dayton, Ralph S. Baric, Raymond J. Pickles, Miriam Braunstein, Nathaniel J. Moorman, Nilu Goonetilleke, and J. Victor Garcia, "Precision mouse models with expanded tropism for human pathogens," National Library of Medicine, https://www.ncbi.nlm.nih.gov/pmc/articles/PMC6776695/.
28. Julie Collorafi, "To Save Ourselves From COVID, We're Sacrificing Children, Part 3: More Baby Parts Are Needed All the Time."
29. Ibid.
30. Julie Collorafi, "LungOnly Mice: Precision Test Models for the COVID Vaccine," HumanizedMice.com, updated November 9, 2021, https://www.humanizedmice.com/post/lungonly-mice-precision-test-models-for-the-covid-vaccine.
31. Angela Wahl, Lisa Gralinski, Claire Johnson, Wenbo Yao, Martina Kovarova, Kenneth Dinnon, Hongwei Liu, Victoria Madden, Halina Krzystek, Chandrav De, Kristen White, Kendra Gully, Alexandra Schäfer, Tanzila Zaman, Sarah Leist, Paul Grant, Gregory Bluemling, Alexander Kolykhalov, Michael Natchus, J. Garcia, "SARS-CoV-2 infection is effectively treated and prevented by EIDD-2801," Nature, 591. 10.1038/s41586-021-03312-w, https://www.researchgate.net/publication/349172933_SARS-CoV-2_infection_is_effectively_treated_and_prevented_by_EIDD-2801.
32. Tara Sander Lee and David Prentice, "A Grim Reminder That Fetal Tissue Market Is Still Open for Business," The Daily Signal, March 4, 2021, https://www.dailysignal.com/2021/03/04/a-grim-reminder-that-fetal-tissue-market-is-still-open-for-business/.
33. Jimmy Tobias, "Evolution of a Theory: Unredacted NIH Emails Show Efforts to Rule Out Lab Origin of Covid," The Intercept, January 9, 2023, https://theintercept.com/2023/01/19/covid-origin-nih-emails/.

34. Taken from Peter Heck, "Christian writers, preachers, and organizations that promoted Francis Collins should break their silence," Not the Bee, February 29, 2022, https://notthebee.com/article/christian-writers-preachers-and-organizations-that-promoted-francis-collins-should-break-their-silence. However, see also Megan Basham, "How The Federal Government Used Evangelical Leaders To Spread Covid Propaganda To Churches," The Daily Wire, n.d., https://www.dailywire.com/news/how-the-federal-government-used-evangelical-leaders-to-spread-covid-propaganda-to-churches.
35. Francis S. Collins, Amy Bany Adams, Courtney Aklin, et al., "Affirming NIH's commitment to addressing structural racism in the biomedical research enterprise," *Cell*, Vol. 184, Issue 12, June 10, 2021, 3075–3079, https://www.cell.com/cell/fulltext/S0092-8674(21)00631-0?_returnURL=https%3A%2F%2Flinkinghub.elsevier.com%2Fretrieve%2Fpii%2FS0092867421006310%3Fshowall%3Dtrue.
36. Francis Collins, "From the NIH Director: NIH 2021 Pride Month," NIH, June 4, 2021, https://www.edi.nih.gov/blog/news/nih-director-nih-2021-pride-month.
37. Darryl G. Hart, "What Was the Modernist-Fundamentalist Controversy?" Reformed Forum, July 7, 2022, https://reformedforum.org/what-was-the-modernist-fundamentalist-controversy/.
38. Gordon-Conwell Theological Seminary, Fuller Seminary, *Christianity Today* magazine, and the National Association of Evangelicals were all either formed or founded as bulwarks to secure the cultural impact desired by neo-evangelicalism's architects.
39. *Time*, July 3, 2000.
40. Russell Moore (@drmoore), "I admire greatly the wisdom, expertise, and, most of all, the Christian humility and grace of Francis Collins," Twitter, October 5, 2021, https://twitter.com/drmoore/status/1445363320089944064?s=20.
41. Joy Allmond, "Evangelicals for Life: Day 2," The Ethics and Religious Liberty Commission, January 28, 2017, https://erlc.com/resource-library/articles/evangelicals-for-life-day-2/.
42. Eugene Cho, "The Abortion Conversation," EugeneCho.com, October 30, 2008, https://eugenecho.com/2008/10/30/the-abortion-conversation/.
43. "HHS Partnership Center Special Feature: Dr. Francis Collins + Pastor Rick Warren," YouTube video, 1:06:58, November 19, 2020, https://www.youtube.com/watch?v=Lz-WMXld0rk&t=0s.
44. David French (@DavidAFrench), "Francis Collins is a national treasure," Twitter, October 5, 2021, https://twitter.com/DavidAFrench/status/1445400222780301321.
45. Michael Gerson, "NIH's Francis Collins, on covid, science and faith: 'There is such a thing as truth'," October 7, 2021, https://www.washingtonpost.com/opinions/2021/10/07/francis-collins-nih-covid-science-faith-truth/.
46. Ed Stetzer, "On Christians Spreading Corona Conspiracies: Gullibility is not a Spiritual Gift," The Exchange with Ed Stetzer, *Christianity Today*, April 15, 2020, https://www.christianitytoday.com/edstetzer/2020/april/christians-and-corona-conspiracies.html.
47. However, thanks to the Internet Archive, as of this writing, it can still be accessed here: https://web.archive.org/web/20200416092325/https:/www.christianitytoday.com/edstetzer/2020/april/christians-and-corona-conspiracies.html.

48. Matt Ridley and Alina Chan, "The Covid Lab-Leak Deception," *The Wall Street Journal*, July 26, 2023, https://www.wsj.com/articles/the-covid-lab-leak-deception-andersen-nih-research-paper-private-message-52fc0c16.
49. For our full discussion, please see "'Just Preach The Gospel' Was Hitler's Favorite Phrase Too | Guest: Eric Metaxas," YouTube video, 32:42, October 19, 2022, https://www.youtube.com/watch?v=Q68up7u_czc&t=1277s.

7. THE DIVINE TRAJECTORY OF GOD'S PEOPLE

1. Many of the stories in this chapter were brought to my attention by George Grant's phenomenal book *Third Time Around* (Brentwood, TN: Wolgemuth & Hyatt, Publishers, Inc., 1991).
2. Sadly, in the Catacomb of Praetextatus in Rome, there is a slave's grave marked with the name "Stercorius." Some have attempted to translate the Latin name as "abandoned in the garbage," but more likely, the correct translation is "little shit." I mention this to illustrate just how unwanted these children were, and how cruel the hearts of their pagan parents could be. See Early Church History editors, "Infanticide in the Ancient World," Early Church History, accessed February 10, 2024, https://earlychurchhistory.org/medicine/infanticide-in-the-ancient-world/.
3. George Grant, "An Unpopular Vision," *Tabletalk*, Feb 1, 2010, https://www.ligonier.org/learn/articles/unpopular-vision.
4. Booker T. Washington, "The Atlanta Exposition Address," September 18, 1895, quoted in History.com editors, "Booker T. Washington," History, updated December 18, 2023, https://www.history.com/topics/black-history/booker-t-washington.
5. Quoted in Marvin Olasky, *The Press and Abortion, 1838-1988* (Hillsdale, NJ: Lawrence Erlbaum Associates, Publishers, 1988), 28.
6. Quoted in *The Christian Monitor*, July 18, 1868.
7. Anna Bowden, Missionary Journals (London: Sunday Schools Association for Overseas Missions, 1896), 1:11, as quoted in Grant, *Third Time Around*.
8. Scott McFetridge and Jim Salter, "Former Mississippi House candidate charged after Satanic Temple display is destroyed at Iowa Capitol," Associated Press, December 15, 2023, https://apnews.com/article/satanic-temple-display-vandalized-iowa-capitol-199fb41983a3f3a390b7be370214bb64.
9. Quinn Hilyer, "Opposing Satan is not a hate crime," *Washington Examiner*, February 1, 2024, https://www.washingtonexaminer.com/opinion/2831891/opposing-satan-is-not-a-hate-crime/.
10. "Man who beheaded satanic statue at state capitol speaks out: 'Righteous indignation'," YouTube video, 4:08, December 15, 2023, https://www.youtube.com/watch?v=ZOkpAR5VHOo.

8. THE WHITE ROSE RESISTANCE 1.0

1. Annette Dumbach & Jud Newborn, *Sophie Scholl and the White Rose* (London: Oneworld Publications, 2018), 193.
2. Ibid., 194-195.

3. Ibid., 148.
4. Ibid., 151.
5. Ibid.
6. Ibid.
7. Don Schwager, ed., "Courage Forged Under Fire," *Living Bulwark*, September 2010, vol. 42, https://livingbulwark.net/wp-content/bulwark/sep10p4.htm.
8. Jacob G. Hornberger, "Holocaust Resistance: The White Rose—A Lesson in Dissent," Jewish Virtual Library, accessed March 9, 2024, https://www.jewishvirtuallibrary.org/the-white-rose-a-lesson-in-dissent.
9. Alabama Chanin editors, "#ThoseWhoInspire: Sophie Scholl," March 21, 2018, Alabama Chanin, https://alabamachanin.com/journal/2018/03/womenwhoinspire-sophie-scholl#.
10. Ibid.
11. Richard Dahlstrom, O^2: *Breathing New Life Into Faith* (Eugene, OR: Harvest House Publishers, 2008), 63.
12. Paul Shrimpton, *Conscience Before Conformity: Hans and Sophie Scholl and the White Rose Resistance in Nazi Germany* (Leominster, UK: Gracewing, 2018), 255. (All quotes from the account of the Scholls's parents attempting and succeeding to enter the courtroom are recorded on page 255.).
13. Ibid., 256-257 (All quotes from the account of Hans and Sophie saying goodbye to their parents are recorded on pp. 256-257.).
14. Jacob G. Hornberger, "Holocaust Resistance: The White Rose—A Lesson in Dissent."
15. Ibid.
16. Inge Scholl, *The White Rose: Munich 1942-1943* (Middletown: Wesleyan University Press, 1983), 56.
17. Dumbach & Newborn, *Sophie Scholl and the White Rose*, 155-156.
18. Ibid., 7.
19. Ibid., 10.

9. SAVED BUT NOT SALTY

1. C. S. Lewis, *The Screwtape Letters* (1961; repr. New York: Simon & Schuster, 1996), 57.
2. Ibid., 148.
3. Martin Niemöller, poetic form of 1946 confessional prose, United States Holocaust Memorial Museum.
4. Eberhard Bethge, *Friendship and Resistance: Essays on Dietrich Bonhoeffer*, (Grand Rapids: Eerdmans, 1995), 24.
5. Anna North, "How abortion became a partisan issue in America," Vox, April 10, 2019, https://www.vox.com/2019/4/10/18295513/abortion-2020-roe-joe-biden-democrats-republicans.
6. Valerie Richardson, "Pro-life doctors challenge threat to certification over abortion 'misinformation,'" *The Washington Times*, August 2, 2022, https://www.washingtontimes.com/news/2022/aug/2/pro-life-doctors-challenge-threat-certification-ov/.

7. Personal text message from Rob McCoy, October 6, 2021.
8. G. K. Chesterton, *What I Saw in America* (New York: Dodd Mead and Company, 1923), 128.

Printed in the USA
CPSIA information can be obtained
at www.ICGtesting.com
CBHW020741170824
13237CB00001B/1/J